THE LIFE AND DEATH OF MY MOTHER

The Life
and Death
of My Mother

ALLEN WHEELIS

W. W. Norton & Company
New York · London

The text of this book is composed in Bembo, with the display
set in Bembo italic.
Composition and Manufacturing by the
Haddon Craftsmen Inc.
Book design by Charlotte Staub.
First Edition.

Library of Congress Cataloging-in-Publication Data

Wheelis, Allen, 1915–
The life and death of my mother/Allen Wheelis.
p.   cm.
I. Title.
PS3573.H44L5   1992
813'.54—dc20   91–2798

ISBN 0-393-03067-9

W. W. Norton & Company, Inc.
500 Fifth Avenue, New York, N.Y. 10110
W. W. Norton & Company, Ltd.
10 Coptic Street, London WC1A 1PU
1 2 3 4 5 6 7 8 9 0

for Vicki

Contents

And so it stays just on the edge of vision,
A small unfocused blur, a standing chill
That slows each impulse down to indecision.
Most things may never happen: this one will.

—*Philip Larkin*

THE LIFE AND DEATH OF MY MOTHER

The
Hidden
Piano

There is a fecal smell in this room. On the bed, unconscious, my mother is slowly bleeding to death from the bowel. Over the radio, faintly, Mahler's Fourth Symphony. I have switched off the light. Outside the window the shadowy gestures of poplars.

Daylight says life is knowable, night tells the truth, says we know not what lies hidden, neither in the darkness out there nor the darkness within. Day is pragmatic acceptance, night is infinite longing.

All of life is here: the smell of shit, the sound of music, the surrounding dark.

WE LOOK INTO the deaths of others, even much-loved others, as in a dark mirror. We seek a glimpse of our own.

15

MY MOTHER IS one hundred years old, has been dying for a long time. For years. Two months ago I was called by the nursing home; that was perhaps the beginning of the end.

She has stopped eating, the nurse tells me. She sits at the table in her wheelchair, pushes the food about with her spoon. If the nurses put it in her mouth she spits it out. If they persist she becomes cross. Occasionally she will swallow a few bites of ice cream. I speak to her on the telephone: "I am coming to see you soon, Mother. I *want* you to eat. Are you listening? Mother? You *must* eat—so you will be strong for my visit." A few days later a call from her doctor: She has lost a lot of weight, he wants to hospitalize her, to begin force-feeding. I refuse. She is confused, I tell him, could not possibly understand what was being done to her, would be terrified by the tube in her throat. I speak again to the nurses: "Offer her small amounts. Frequently. Encourage her to eat. But don't force her." I try to speak to her on the phone, hear the nurse say, "Hold it to your ear, Mrs. Wheelis. It's your son!" "Mother!" I yell into the phone. "Mother! Can you hear me?" She drops the phone in her lap, mumbles unintelligibly.

When I arrive she is not in her room. I glance in the open door. Her blue mohair shawl lies in a heap on the bed. I go looking for her—in the halls, in the TV room—return presently to discover that my mother herself lies beneath that crumpled shawl. A tangle of bones in a bag of skin. Her body makes no impression on the bed. I take her hand, call her name, shake her slightly.

The smeared eyes open blankly. "Mother . . . it's me. Your son. It's Allen." Suddenly the skeleton hand tightens on mine, a smile comes to her face. She struggles to lift herself, to turn toward me. She falls back, but presently, out of that waste, two stick arms rise up to embrace me.

I stay with her three days. From my hand, when I command it, she will eat. Constantly I am lifting something to her mouth, urging on her yet another sip of liquid protein. She gains some strength, is able to talk, can sit up for a few minutes.

IN THE PICTURE I sit on my father's knee. I am one year old. Can one say "I" of an infant seventy-three years away? On the other knee my sister, June, five years old. Behind us my mother, a tall slender woman, round face, smooth white skin, heavy dark luxuriant hair coiled loosely at the back of her head in a bun. She wears a white blouse with lace collar. Her folded hands rest on her husband's shoulder. She stands before the empty fireplace, the cold hearth, looks down on her young family. Her expression is enigmatic: proud, shy, perhaps smug. On the mantel a clock, hands frozen for all these years at eight minutes past eleven; it rests on a doily with scalloped border, embroidered flowers, and a message: Daisies Won't Tell. Behind the clock a mirror. My father wears a striped shirt with high white starched collar, dark tie. His Sunday best. He is thirty-four. It is 1916.

My father holds before me his gold watch. I am transfixed with desire, eyes wide and gleaming, face aglow.

Yes, I can say "I" of that infant; I recognize myself in that longing. It's mine still, only now without an object. Then a watch would do, or a bird, or a leaf. The longing now is nameless, voiceless, a burning inward sun.

In the picture my mother, my father, my sister all look at the watch. They are following my rapturous gaze, sharing my experience of a longing that still knows what it wants, something tangible, something right there, within reach. For their separate and mute longings have already submerged, become nameless, as soon will mine. I show them a lost paradise. Try as they will, they will never find it. Nor will I.

My mother is twenty-seven years old. In her climb up out of nothingness, this was perhaps the high point, the crest of consciousness, power, specialness. At this moment, perhaps, her death began. Who could have imagined, then, that she would live seventy-three years more? that it would be downhill all the way?

A YEAR LATER the war swept up her husband, and she followed him with her two children to army camps in Alabama and Mississippi, then to Chattanooga, Tennessee, where she nursed him through a near-fatal illness during the flu epidemic of 1918. In 1919, a free man again, he borrowed money, built a small house in Minden, Louisiana, and began practice as a country doctor. Now they were out of the woods, they thought, now things would get easier. But within months he had tuberculosis. He lay flat in bed and, as the months passed, got worse. He should move to a drier climate, he was

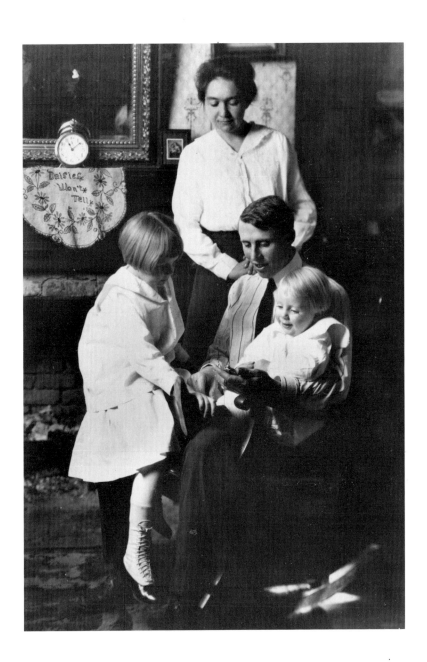

told; so she sold the house and packed up their belongings and moved him and her children to San Antonio. The only treatment, the doctors said, was fresh air and absolute bedrest. He did not want to be in a sanitarium, so she rented a little house, installed him on a screened-in porch where he could be isolated from her children, and began to nurse him: serving meals to him in bed, carrying out the bedpans, boiling the sheets, burning the sputum cups—day after day after day.

THESE ARE the last hours of my mother's life. And she knows nothing. Only I observe her blind, stumbling arrival at the end of a century-long journey. I hope it may be different as I lie dying. I hope that I will be able to take myself as the object of reflection, see my life in extension, the whole course—taking off like a ballistic missile, soaring, leveling off, falling—and, just before the end, achieve, like the computer in a warhead at impact, a view of the whole trajectory.

I doubt my mother has ever done this, or would want to. For years now, she has had no awareness of death. Death got lost as memory failed and reality slipped away. The last time she grappled with it was six years ago. She was ninety-four, frail and failing. She took my hand, solemnly, between both of her own, her voice dropped, her manner became portentous. "Son, I want you to know . . . *you* know . . . I don't want to live forever . . . you know that . . . son, some folks nowadays . . . they just hang on and on, no use to themselves or anybody else, taking up space and costing money. I don't want anything like that. I don't want you to take any special measures . . . you know what I mean?"

"Yes, Mama, I know."

"I've lived a long time, and when my time comes . . . when it's right for me to go . . . well . . . I'm ready. I leave that all to you. It's up to you."

"I understand."

"I don't want to just hang on when my mind is gone and I'm no use to people."

"You're still in good health, Mama. You have a lot of life before you. I want you to keep living as long as you can enjoy things."

We sit in silence. She strokes my hand absently, brooding, troubled. Her breathing becomes irregular, she wants to speak. Can't find the right words. She sighs. "Son," she says after a bit, "son . . . tell me . . . how long do you think I will live?"

I realize she is afraid. "You have a lot of vitality, Mother. You've always been very strong. . . ."

"That's true."

"You've pulled through bad sicknesses that would've been too much for most people."

"That's true."

"So I think you might . . . live to . . ." I canvass her anxious face, extend my estimate. ". . . you'll probably live to be one hundred!" Wildly extravagant. But maybe she will buy it. Perhaps it will make her happy.

Her expression doesn't change. She fixes her eyes on mine, judiciously weighs, examines, my estimate: "That's not very long, you know."

IN ATTENDING my mother's death I preview my own, try to get the feel of it, take its measure. But cannot, can never get this matter settled. I accept what's coming only in the sense of acknowledging its inevitability, not in affirming its propriety or rightness.

An uneasy truce, the terms are not clear. Something more should be possible. One should not be stuck forever with this nagging problem as unfinished business. How is it handled by the wise? by the really mature?

An interview on television with Erik Erikson. "And have you achieved wisdom, Mr. Erikson?" The question is loaded, for Erik has staked his reputation on the depiction of life as phasic; and the task of the last phase, in which his shaky infirmity unmistakably places him, presents the alternatives of wisdom and despair. "Have you achieved wisdom, Mr. Erikson?" He hesitates, then stands behind his product: "I'm afraid I have."

Mazeltov. I have not. I'm as old as he, almost. Anyway, like him, slogging along through the last phase, if it *is* a phase, anyway the last years of life. But not with wisdom. Rather with the vanity, awkwardness, longing, and sham that have characterized my passage through all the other phases.

I distrust the wisdom of old men. I listen to them and am not convinced. I suspect a cover-up. They don't have things really straight either. They're headed, mapless, into the same dark that awaits us all.

WE KNOW WHAT it is, we see it lying in wait up ahead: Consciousness is going to end. That vast net which, nearing the end of a long life, has acquired such enormous reach into time and space, such variety of experience, inward and outward, backward and forward, that knows so much, and, beyond what it knows, can imagine anything—consciousness, that ringing glass, is going to shatter, its shards plunge back into nothingness. Like the fading fragments of a burst of fireworks.

ONE BY ONE my mother picks up the pullets, dandles them in her hands, estimating plumpness. Having selected one, she closes the chicken coop and walks some distance away. The pullet rests easily in the palm of her left hand, cranes its neck in curiosity, its legs dangling down between my mother's fingers. The head turns easily on the supple neck, the soft feathers accommodate to the stretch and rotation, the bright button eyes scan the world. With her right hand my mother maintains a soothing and restraining caress of the wings. The bird utters a bemused clucking. Presently that caressing right hand seizes the neck of the bird and carries it down in a violent jerk, then around and up, and suddenly down again, and up again, over and over, in exactly the movement with which my Uncle Kleber cranks the Model T. The body of the chicken follows helplessly after the violent arc of the inexorable hand which spirals to a smaller and faster orbit. Presently the body breaks free and lands ten feet away. The head drops to the ground from my mother's hand. The body now leaps high into the air, wings flapping, blood spurting from the stump of neck. One leap brings it to me, and a row of crimson drops, as if from a minute machine gun, thuds across my arm. With what desperation does this headless creature fight against dying! And with what futility! Each leap is weaker; moment by moment the spurts diminish. Soon there is but a feeble stirring of wings and legs in the dirt, then nothing. My mother picks up the body, takes it into the house.

I squat down by the young lifeless head and try to recognize in it the lithe and supple alertness of but moments past. The bright button eyes are now glazed and dusty. After a while my sister emerges from the house carrying on a piece of newspaper the unwanted smoking remains. She squats beside me, spills them out on the ground. Together we examine the bloody innards. With a small stick my sister gingerly pushes at the entrails, which, to our amazement, respond with a slow twisting movement. When she presses harder the movement increases, and from the torn end oozes a brown liquid. "That's the do-do," she says. "Ah . . . !" I shudder. That family word, that intimate baby word, makes the connection with me. Do-do issues also from me. My insides must look like this. We are, all of us, full of shit and mortality. Something holy departs from life, leaving me adrift in the same fortuity in which this hapless bird lived and died.

WHAT WE DENY is not death but the awareness that, before we die, nothing is going to happen. That big vague thing, that redemptive fulfillment, is an illusion, a beckoning bribe to keep us loyal. A symphony has a climax, a poem builds to a burst of meaning, but we are unfinished business. No coming together of strands. The game is called because of darkness.

WHEN I DIE I want my body to be cremated, the ashes buried in the orchard on the island in Puget Sound, the site marked by a flat stone of green marble bearing my name and dates, and, a small distance below, my paradox.

> How to live?
> Who knows the question knows not how,
> Who knows not the question cannot tell.

Those three lines sum me up: the inquiry that has driven me, and the impasse into which it has invariably delivered me.

I choose the orchard because there, among those gnarled and broken apple trees, blossoming unseen on the empty air, dropping their wormy and unwanted fruit for the deer and the crows, the loamy land sloping down to the slough, the blue heron standing motionless on one long spindly leg, mirrored in the still water, the steely blue Sound beyond, and far away on the horizon the jagged Olympic Mountains, icy, snow-covered, distant—there, at times, I've had a sense of home.

Actually I would prefer to be buried there, my body intact, in a plain cedar box. But that's hard to arrange; and, as between lying intact among strangers in a cemetery or lying in ashes and bone fragments in that magical place, I choose the latter.

And I can see it coming about. Soon. I shall not have long to wait. And when it is done, my wishes all exactly met by a loving and respectful family, it will gratify me not at all; for the consciousness that now wills it and is capable of gratification by it shall have vanished. Indeed, it would matter naught to me, at that time, were my body thrown into the garbage. I am carefully arranging something that cannot possibly become a reality until its purpose and fulfillment shall have become unknowable to me. So any brooding on that site, any ghostly gratification, must be claimed in advance. Now.

So . . . this is the future scene to which I suppose I am now laying claim. A late summer afternoon, the sun disappearing behind the Olympics, the sawtooth ridge knifelike against a pale green sky, clouds red and gold, becoming pink turning to gray turning to black. Far far overhead, silently, a plane passes, leaving a glittering silver trail. A sloop with a blue sail glides past the beach. The heron rises ponderously from the slough, the great wings beating slowly, heavily, uttering his hoarse and protesting cry. From the table at the edge of the cliff near the house come voices, the sounds of dinner—my children and grandchildren, friends, dogs. Joan wanders alone down through the twilit orchard, glances at the green stone, reads again the pithy anguish of my life. I always wanted to write in stone: now I will have done so. She directs toward me a current of melancholy affection, reexperiences the quite special bond between us. The stone is partly covered by the long dry grass of autumn. I must clear that away, she thinks . . . plant some flowers. Perhaps tomorrow. She glances . . . and passes on . . . and that's all.

So—I can imagine all this. And my mother cannot. Does that make any difference?

Night falls.

That's all.

FIVE YEARS OLD, too young for school. Skinny arms and legs sticking out from skimpy pants and short-sleeve shirt. When the older boys got back from school I went to Jimmy's house to play. Five boys had arranged themselves in a circle, were throwing a ball one to another in sequence. I put myself in the circle, but when my turn came the ball sailed over my head to the next in line. An oversight, perhaps; I waited the next round. When passed over again, I complained. They did not seem to hear. My complaint grew louder, became pleading. Again and again the ball flew over my head. I jumped but could not reach it, wailed, went to my friend who usually was willing to play with me, tugged on his sleeve, "Let me play, Jimmy! Throw it to me too! Please, Jimmy!" Jimmy shrugged, threw the ball over my head. I began to cry. "It's not fair!" I was enraged, wanted to retaliate, to walk away. But could not reject them so long as they would not see me, would not hear. And because they were denying my existence I could not give up trying to enter their circle. I began to run after the ball, tried to intercept throws, but when I managed to position myself before the next receiver, the order would change, the ball going instead to someone else. I ran back and forth, in and out, never finding a way to become a part. It was a magic circle, it joined them, excluded me. I was a nonperson.

Eventually I gave up, sat down at some distance, exhausted, disheartened, watched the ball fly around, one to another, in sequences of infinite desirability. It was too painful to watch, I lowered my head, scratched in the dirt. When my crying stopped, the boys tired of the game, stood about idly, bored, wondered what to do next. "Here, Allen," Jimmy said, as if to a dog, and tossed me the now unwanted ball. The boys huddled, came to a decision, set off together. "Where are we going?" I asked, following after. But again could not make myself heard. I ran to keep up, but they ran faster, and came presently to a thicket which, with their long pants, they could push through, whereas I, with bare legs, was turned back bleeding. The boys disappeared, their laughter grew fainter, died away. I extricated myself from the brush, walked back toward Jimmy's house. It was getting dark. There was a strong and cold wind. I was whimpering. Maybe crying.

Then there was my mother standing before me in her long brown coat. "A norther has come up," she said, taking my hand. "All of a sudden. That's why it's so dark and cold." I looked up. Black clouds were rushing across the sky. She wiped my nose. "We must go home." The pebbles hurt my bare feet; I hopped and lurched, holding her hand, trying to avoid the sharper stones. My teeth were chattering, the skin of my arms and legs became goose flesh. My mother stopped, opened her coat.

"Come inside," she said. She folded me into the coat, buttoned it in front of me. We proceeded awkwardly, my shoulder against her thigh, my head alongside her hip, enveloped in darkness, in warmth, in the smell of her body. She was wearing an apron, and there was a smell also of food—onions and something fried. She must have been cooking supper when the norther hit. And stopped to come get me.

It was difficult to walk; we went slowly. I couldn't see anything ahead, but looking down could see the ground where I was putting my feet. I was getting warm in that germinal darkness. My teeth stopped chattering, my knees stopped shaking. I was aware of the powerful movement of her hip against my cheek, the sense of a large bone moving under strong muscles. Aware also that it was difficult for her to walk with me buttoned in. Occasionally she stumbled. And just then, for the first time, I became aware of goodness. Of goodness as a special quality, like evil, which a person may or may not possess. She doesn't *have* to do this, I thought. It's not necessary. I'm cold, but I could make it home all right.

What she gave me could not have been demanded; I would never have thought to ask. All afternoon I had been demanding something to which it seemed I had a right, and had been denied; yet here was a good to which I had no right, freely offered. No trade. Nothing asked in return.

WHEN I WAS FIVE my father improved, blood disappeared from his sputum, he was in high spirits, was getting well. For the first time I saw him up and about, in ordinary clothes. My mother was blooming. Foreboding drained from her face, color rushed in, she had never been so pretty. My father bought a Maxwell touring car, we went driving through the countryside, and when it rained we snapped on the isinglass window curtains. It was about this time, too, my mother agreed to call Tall Betsy.

Tall Betsy was perhaps eight feet tall, with long willowy arms. No one had ever seen her face. From the top of her head to the ground she was clothed in trailing white robes. She did not speak, but uttered wailing cries and sharp growls. Sometimes on a cold, windy night I would hear from far away a sound such as might be made by a woman in pain, and would start up with alarm. "What's that?" And my mother would answer, "That's Tall Betsy," and I would wait anxiously for the cry to be repeated. Sometimes I would ask, "Mama, doesn't she get cold out there in the woods?" And my mother would answer confidently, "No, she doesn't mind the cold in winter or the heat in summer."

Tall Betsy had never been seen except at night; no one knew where she stayed by day. Very likely, I thought, she made herself invisible or changed into a stump. I had often looked for her in caves or gullies or hollow trees, both longing to find her and relieved I did not. Sometimes at night, however, she would come out of the woods, and even enter our yard. Apparently my mother had an understanding with her; for when my mother called she would come. Tall Betsy, my father once said, roamed all over the world, but loved my mother with a pure and ghostly love, and no matter how far away she might be—even in China—she would always come when my mother called.

But Tall Betsy was more than a ghost, and more than a game, she was also a threat, a lurking menace, an unbearable loss. For if, when my mother was exhausted and harassed, I added to her strain and her troubles by importuning or misbehaving, her patience would crack, and she would cry out, "I can't stand it any longer! I just can't! I can't! I'm going away to the woods and live with Tall Betsy!" And a spiraling pain would twist down in my heart.

Dinner is over, my father is polishing the Maxwell, I am helping my mother with the dishes. I am eager for her to be finished, for she has already agreed to call Tall Betsy. Bill Evans calls from the front of the house. Soon other children arrive. Bob Johnson, the two Miller boys with their dog, Sarge, and others. We sit on the porch in the twilight and talk in hushed tones, speculate about the creature we are about to see. Is she a ghost or just an old woman who lives in the woods? As dusk changes to night we become tense and expectant, the younger boys glancing apprehensively at the edge of the woods about fifty yards away. Sarge howls, and a shiver passes through us. Bob says he once saw Tall Betsy in the daytime, but Tom Evans says no, that she can't be seen in daylight. I then tell them (making it up as I go along) that my father said that Tall Betsy once carried off a little boy, and the whole town searched the woods for weeks, but no trace was ever found; it stands to reason, then, that if Tall Betsy gets hold of you "you are a goner."

After a while my mother comes out with a lamp and sits on the porch with us. We beg her to call right away, but she says we must wait, that Tall Betsy never comes before dark. We ply her with questions; her answers are cryptic and evasive. We must not approach too closely, we are not to throw stones. Tom volunteers that if you do, Tall Betsy will set your house on fire.

Night has come now. There are ten of us sitting on the steps, waiting. We become quiet and listen intently. The hum of crickets and the croaking of frogs are the only sounds. The blackness of night is sequined with fireflies.

"Call her now, Mama!"

"All right. But she may not come, you know." She walks out in the darkness where she is visible to us only as a blur. We marvel at her bravery. As for ourselves, we stay near the porch, so we can run into the house if Tall Betsy comes too close. When my mother reaches the woods she stops and in a high voice begins to call.

"Tall . . . ll . . . Bet . . . tsy!"

We are tensely quiet, we look about. No telling where she might appear. Perhaps right beside us. Minutes pass. No one speaks. The silence and uncertainty build such suspense that we are ready, equally, to laugh or run or cry. After a while my mother tries again. A high-pitched, tremulous, singing call.

"Tall . . . ll . . . Bet . . . tsy!"

Again we wait, half in hope, half in fear, my mother's

plaintive call lingering in the air. When another span of foreboding silence has passed, someone says, "Maybe she won't come." But just as we begin to breathe easier, we are chilled by a manic cry. "That's her! That's Tall Betsy!" I shout. "Where? Where is she?" "I don't see her." "I don't know," I say, "but that was her all right! She made that sound!"

We look in all directions, see nothing. As the waiting continues, some of the more daring venture away from the house, among them I. I feel that, in a sense, it is my game, it belongs to me, and so am determined to play a major part. Presently one of us sees what all are looking for.

"There she is! By that tree!"

"That white thing?"

"Yes, that her!"

"It's not moving."

"It moved just a minute ago. That's her all right."

Then a long, lonely wailing.

"There! That's where it came from!"

"Look! It's moving!"

"That's her! That's Tall Betsy!"

At first we see only a white haze which, as we watch, slowly approaches. We group together, watch in silence. All are afraid. She is the tallest living thing we ever have seen, as tall as the mesquite trees from which she eerily emerges. Her arms are proportionately long, and she waves them in a sinuous, uncanny motion. No one can see her face, or indeed, even know that she has one. She seems to consist entirely of flowing white drapery. Her approach takes a long time; for she weaves slowly back and forth, occasionally emitting the awful cry. As there seems to be no immediate danger, I compose myself sufficiently to call out. "Hey! Tall Betsy! I'm not afraid of you!" On being so addressed, she stops, growls, takes a few quick steps in our direction. There is a sharp intake of breath among us.

"If you are not afraid," Bob says, "why don't you go on out there?"

"All right, I will. Come get me, Tall Betsy! I'm not afraid of you!"

The apparition growls again and makes a dash for me. The girls shriek, the boys laugh nervously, and the group breaks up, everyone running and yelling in excitement. Despite her height Tall Betsy is not fast, and all but the youngest can outrun her. One of us provokes her to give chase and then flees, laughing and screaming, until someone else can command her attention and malice.

"I bet you can't catch me, Tall Betsy!"

"I'm not afraid of any old ghost!"

"I could lick ten Tall Betsies!"

"You'd better not set my house on fire. I'll beat the tar out of you!"

"Don't catch me, Tall Betsy. I'll kick you in the pants!"

Yet all of us run when she gives chase.

Presently, as I am standing in the outer fringe of the group, resting from a sortie, Tall Betsy suddenly, without warning or provocation, singles me out. She points her long arm, growls, and dashes for me at top speed. I turn and flee, escaping her grasp, but to my dismay find that she is between me and the house. Unable to elude her by running to either side, I am forced to enter the woods, and there, in the blackness, out of sight of the house, I am terrified. Stumbling, in panic, scratched by thorns, I manage to escape her, come upon a back road, and reach home from a different direction. There I find that Tall Betsy has returned and that the game is going on without me. Forced to sit down to rest and compose myself, I resolve to be more cautious.

It was wonderful fun, being chased by a spook, and we could have played it all night. Tall Betsy tires of it, however; and after an hour of snarling and chasing she begins to retreat, weaving and swaying in her ghostly fashion. And as she moves further from the lamp on the porch we become less willing to go near her. When she reaches the woods she makes beckoning gestures to my mother. Having ignored her throughout the game, she now seems eager that my mother come to her.

"Look!" Tom says. "She's signaling!"

"What's she trying to do?"

"Allen's mother is going to her!"

"She's hypnotized!"

My mother responds hesitantly, approaching a few steps at a time. While the others watch with interest, I watch with alarm.

"Mama!" She stops and looks back wonderingly. "Mama! Come back!"

As if weighing the two invitations, she looks again at

Tall Betsy, whose gestures have become more imperative.

"Mama! . . . Mama! Come back!"

With a last look at me she yields to the wraith, goes forward until Tall Betsy's long arm reaches out and takes her hand.

"Mama!" I cry.

Now she does not look back. The two slowly enter the woods. In desperation I run to them and catch my mother's free hand in both my own. The closeness to Tall Betsy terrifies me, but the thought of losing my mother is unbearable. Trying to keep her between me and Tall Betsy, I pull on her arm and plead. "Mama! Come back!"

As if in a trance she stops, turns to me, and says, "Tall Betsy wants me to go away to the woods and live with her."

"Don't go, Mama! Don't go. Please!"

As my mother stands there undecided, Tall Betsy becomes impatient and tries to drag her. I hold firm, and no progress is made. Irritated by my opposition, the ghost snarls and flails at me. I try to dodge the unnaturally long arms while clinging desperately to my mother and trying to draw her away. "Mama! *Please!*"

"Well . . . I don't know."

"Mama!" I scream, my voice cracking.

She squeezes my hand. "All right, hon. Don't cry." Then, to the ghost, she says, "I guess I can't go with you tonight."

Tall Betsy receives this with a spasm of anger, but my mother and I begin walking back toward the house. I keep looking over my shoulder in case we should be pursued and hold tight to my mother lest she change her mind. Ignoring the curious glances of the other children, I hold on to her hand long after we reach the porch, to be sure she stays.

For a while longer Tall Betsy can be seen weaving about in the edge of the woods, now appearing, now disappearing, while we sit on the steps and watch. Finally she disappears entirely, but still for a while we hear her cry, gradually becoming more distant. When heard no more the game is over and the other children begin, apprehensively, reluctantly, to leave. They depart in groups, staying close to the middle of the road.

When all are gone my mother and I enter the house. My father is sitting in the kitchen by a lamp, breathing heavily. Sweat stands out on his face.

"Daddy," I say excitedly, "you should have come out. Tall Betsy almost pulled Mama away into the woods!"

He does not reply, and there is something in his expression that makes me fall silent. Mama sits down across the room from him, I by her side.

"Well . . ." she says, but there is no response and she does not continue.

She holds me close and strokes my hair. I am uncomfortable looking at my father, hide my face on her shoulder. A heavy silence hangs in the room.

MY FATHER'S RECOVERY proved but a brief remission. Within a month the racking cough returned, and the bloody sputum. He sold the Maxwell, fell back in bed, back in pajamas, resumed the downward slide of tuberculosis.

ONCE A WEEK an iron pot hangs from a tripod over a wood fire. My father watches from the house. When the water comes to a boil my mother puts in the sheets, tells me to stir, and I poke at them with a broom handle, driving them down, and they gurgle and foam and surge upward, ever more violently, steam rising, swaying, swirling around me, the fire getting hotter, my face burning, sweat dripping. My mother then removes the sheets with the broom handle, throws them over the clothesline, empties the pot, removes the tripod. "Go inside now," she says.

From the house my father and I watch as she spreads the fire and then, one by one, carefully, places the accumulated sputum cups in the bed of red-hot coals.

"I like to see them burn," my father says.

Sometimes three or four, sometimes seven or eight, white waxed cardboard boxes, each filled with thick mucus, yellow and green and red—my father's inner substance—lined up one after another in the seething fire, a train of little coffins describing my father's downhill slide through the week.

"Millions of tubercle bacilli," my father says. "Maybe

billions. They're eating my lungs out. They are going to kill me."

Suddenly he cries out: "The sputum is putting out the fire! Build it up, son! Pile on more wood!"

I rush outside. "Keep away!" my mother says.

"But Daddy . . ."

"Stand back!" she says abruptly. "These things explode, splatter germs."

She herself adds the wood, while I go back inside. I am in thrall to my father's despair. From the window he watches with manic stare. "Out there," he murmurs, "I can destroy them. But in here . . ." He taps his chest, presently turns on me accusingly. "If I could just *get inside,* in here"—he taps his chest more urgently—"and scratch out the cavities, clean them out with a knife . . . then paint the walls with iodine . . ."

I have the sense of being addressed, not as a child, not as a son, but as a mysterious stranger. I am being made to bear witness to his case against God.

A PAROXYSM of coughing throws him forward, half upright in bed, rocks him back and forth, side to side. He grabs the sputum cup, holds it to his mouth. Blood and purulent mucus gush forth. He supports himself on his left elbow as, gradually, the spell subsides. He replaces the cup on the bedside table, lifts the covers, looks down the length of his body—gaunt, heaving rib cage, sunken belly, stick legs, and, springing up from this wasteland, obelisk in the desert, a gigantic erection. He sees me looking from the doorway, drops the covers. I watch the somber eyes look me over, take me into account; those eyes, I think, are meditating that I will live while he will die. "Go back to your work, son."

In the evening when the chores are done, my mother sits with him, mending clothes. The light fails, the summer evening turns to dusk, to night. He is very weak, does not move, can hardly speak. She lays aside her sewing, turns on the light, stands beside the bed, looks down at him, takes his hand. He looks up at her in pain and foreboding. She is frightened, tries to control it, to deny it. She sits again, rocks slightly. She is terrified of being alone.

A still night, not a breath of air. The faint hum of insects. A deep silence. Suddenly a violent flurry of feathers. She starts, jumps up. Gray wings are beating on the screen wire. Claws and tawny beadlike eyes appear for a moment. Then nothing. That deep silence again. She turns to him. A messenger, she thinks, then denies it: "It's so sultry . . . there'll be a storm."

Again she moves to the bed, stands beside him. He turns aside his head. "Look at me," she says. "Can I do something for you?" Slowly he moves his head side to side. "I want you to feel better. I want you to get strong again."

He looks up at her from a deep well. She is a reed, will fall to the first man who lays hands on her. "I would feel better," he whispers, "if I knew . . . that you . . . would not marry again."

She is astonished: "I want you to get *well!*"

He brushes this aside. "Promise me: When I die . . . you will not . . . marry again." His bony fingers sink into her flesh.

"I promise," she says.

AS MY FATHER SANK into darkness my world filled with light.

Before sunrise, someone tugging at my sleeve. "Wake up! Wake up!" my sister whispers. "Daddy's real sick." Shadowy figures, edged in lamplight, hover about the bed. Dr. Whittaker leans forward, motionless, stethoscope to my father's chest. Behind him, leaning forward in the same curve of frozen apprehension, my mother seems to hold her breath. Minutes pass. Nothing happens. Nothing, I think, will happen. My father is often "real sick."

Now I make out the figures of Mr. and Mrs. Means in the shadows, motionless, listening. My sister stands in the doorway. The room becomes strangely purple. I look from one to another of the still, waiting faces. A slight tint of pink now touches these faces, then a wave of light washes up around us. I turn, catch the first rim of sun slicing up through the horizon, into the pale green sky. The air around us becomes more strongly pink. Still nothing happens. Then, suddenly, a horizontal beam of golden light flashes across the room, splatters on the porcelain music box, splinters on the stethoscope, the clock, becomes incandescent in my mother's dark hair. Dr. Whittaker slowly straightens up, folds the stethoscope, turns. My mother, mouth open, eyes wide with agony, strains against what's coming. "He's gone." She flinches as if to a whip, a shudder sweeps across her body, she reels back uttering a scream so loud, so hoarse, of such deep pain, the scream of a large animal that has been struck a mortal blow—a scream that tears through me like a spear, that I hear still in the roots of my teeth.

A FEW DAYS later, at noon, the brilliant light falling vertically in golden shafts, and all around us the intense green of the grass, the red and yellow of roses set in vases before the gray stones, the purple of peonies and pink oleander, and above us the light green of the leaves, and overall the clear blue sky. Amidst all this color we make our way, about thirty of us, through the cemetery.

My mother walks slowly, I on one side holding her hand, my sister on the other. We seat ourselves in the first row of folding chairs. Directly before us is a trestle of steel on which black-suited men now place the coffin. People arrive slowly, seating themselves behind us, the minister taking a stand to one side, the funeral director folding back the upper half of the coffin lid. My father is clad in a navy-blue suit, white shirt, dark tie. A stranger. I have trouble recognizing him, knew him only in the gray pajamas of illness. The eyes that have seen through me all these years are closed, the face that relentlessly condemned my flawed and wayward character is waxen and still—pointed upward, almost as if straining upward, to escape the coffin, dignified but helpless, the long thin nose like the keel of an upturned ship.

Beneath the steel trestle is a green cloth simulating

grass. It is sagging, thereby revealing the grave it is meant to deny. Two black-suited men stretch it taut. The minister places a hymn book on the music stand, raises his arms. "Brethren . . . let us harken to the words of our Savior Jesus Christ."

Directly behind the coffin is something standing up vertically, about five feet high, covered with a green felt cloth. I turn to my Aunt Mit on my left, whisper, "What is that?" and point. "Shhhh," she says. " 'Let not your heart be troubled,' " the minister intones, " 'ye believe in God, believe also in me.' " I turn to my mother, touch her arm. Her lips are moving. The minister continues: " 'In my Father's house are many mansions: if it were not so, I would have told you. I go to prepare a place for you. And if I go and prepare a place for you, I will come again, and receive you unto myself; that where I am, there ye may be also. And whither I go ye know, and the way ye know.' " "Mama," I whisper, "Mama, is that thing . . . a piano?" I point at the green mound. "Shhhh," she whispers. Her eyes are red, tears run down her face, dropping in her lap. In the brilliant light I see the fine hair at the line of her chin, the tear detained in that hair. The glare makes me squint. The sun is beating on the blue sky as on a drum. The heat falls in waves. I itch and squirm in my wool jacket.

At a gesture we stand. The minister closes his eyes, recites a prayer, raising his voice as if to loft the prayer heavenward.

It *is* a piano, I decide. It is exactly the shape of the upright piano in our church, and is covered by the same green felt. That slight bulge about the middle is the key-board. Presently, the minister will pull off the cover and someone will play. Maybe my mother will play. When they lower the body into the grave . . . that's when . . . *then* she will play. Maybe "After the Ball Is Over' or "The Burning of Rome." Another prayer. Then we are asked to stand to sing a hymn. *Now,* I think, now they will take off the cover. The hymn is finished. We sit again. Then another prayer.

And then, suddenly, it is over. My mother is ap-proaching the coffin, leading me by the hand. Someone holds out to her a paper bag of rose petals. She takes a few, drops them on the coffin. We move on. Looking back, I see others doing the same, one after another, putting their hands in the bag, taking out the rose petals, dropping them on the coffin. Now we are walking down the path. "Isn't anybody going to play the piano?" I ask, and my mother bursts into sobs. In the limousine I try once more. "Mama . . . what was that green thing? What was under that green cloth? Was it a piano?" "No . . ." Her eyes are dry and bleak, look over me to a desolate future. "It was . . . dirt . . . to fill the grave."

Good-By, Mama

Downtown San Antonio. An old man with a push-cart. Dilapidated felt hat, deeply creased with a spreading sweat stain, blue shirt, baggy pants, scraggly salt-and-pepper beard, red nose, pale twinkling eyes under bushy gray eyebrows, a wizened smile and a wink for my mother. Before him a small chopping board, a sizzling grill, buns and pretzels in the glass warming oven. My mother is pondering whether she can afford to buy me a treat.

Seeing us watching, he takes a sausage in his left hand, holds it aloft. Plump as if to burst, thick as a man's arm, red and shining. He lowers it to the board and draws across it a long heavy knife, first in the air as if to savor the cut, then, lowering the edge, he pulls the knife slowly toward himself, hunching his shoulders and sucking in his breath, as a slice of sausage peels away. A lascivious moment, a shudder of relaxation. He impales the slice of sausage on the knife, advances it toward me as if to drop it in my hands, or perhaps to impale me too, all with a droll expression on his mischievous face, then, smoothly rotating his body, drops it on the smoking grill where it sizzles with the spicy aroma of pepper and pork and frying fat.

Amid a flutter of wings a pigeon alights on the cart. With a snakelike sweep of his left hand he scoops up the bird, forces the legs into extension, lowers it to the chopping board. Glancing at me with that mischievous grin, he whacks off the pigeon's feet. With his left hand he throws aloft the shocked bird as, with his right, holding the knife, he brushes to the ground the twitching feet.

My mother utters an anguished cry, clutches me to her, trembles, pulls me away.

At nine I passionately wanted a certain type of scooter. Two wheels in back, one in front, a platform to stand on that tilted forward and back with the shift in one's weight, this movement being translated by gears into the rotation of the rear wheels. We were very poor, my mother and sister and I living on eighty dollars a month; and this scooter, my mother told me, was beyond our means. But I would not give up. I begged, I pleaded, I suggested that we could do without certain other things deemed to be necessities, I made budgets. We didn't have to get it right now, I said, it could be for Christmas. She was going to spend *something* for Christmas anyway. "Please, Mama, don't say no, say at least maybe." So finally, to get some peace, she said, "Well, maybe . . ." and of course that meant yes. So then I pestered her to buy it soon, buy it now, "please, Mama, because if you wait till December they will all be sold." But she does not have the money now. But she could make a deposit, I tell her. Just so they'll hold it. And again, finally, she says, "Well, maybe," which means yes.

But now I wonder: Has she actually done it? She tends to procrastinate. Maybe she's putting it off. So I start in on her about that. Has she actually, *really,* made the deposit? "I can't say," she says. "It's supposed to be for Christmas—isn't it?—*if* you get it? It's supposed to be a *surprise.*" But I want to *know.* I want to be sure. "You don't have to *tell* me," I say to her. "You don't have to say *anything* in words. I'll just ask you, 'Have you already got it?' and *if* you've got it, just move your eyelids a little bit."

She looks at me wonderingly. She is sitting on the back steps of our little house, I standing before her, bare feet in the still-warm earth. Dusk. Around us the empty flatness of Texas. The pink glow of sunset beginning to go purple. She leans forward, elbows on her knees. A pretty woman, still young, alone, poor, insecure, two children . . . and I before her twisting her fingers. *"Please,* Mama!" She gazes at me, her hands inert in my entreating and manipulative grasp. She looks away at the darkening horizon. I wait. And then, slowly, her eyelids flicker.

My father was a despot who rendered me powerless. But with his death I assumed absolute power over my mother.

I LIE ON MY COT on the back porch, sleepless. A summer night. I am drenched in silver light. Silence, stillness. Not a leaf moves. Yet high above there must be a wind, for dark clouds move slowly across the full moon. The air is warm, humid, a smell of honeysuckle. Tornado weather. I push down the covers. The moon gleams its radiant invitation. I sleep briefly, wake with a start. The moon has disappeared. I feel an ache, a distant agitation.

I make my way through the dark house to my mother's room. "Mama." She moves, wakes. "What? What is it?" "I can't sleep, Mama. Can I come in with you?" "Of course you can." She lifts the covers. I climb in beside her, facing the window. She spoons herself behind me, enfolds me in her arms, her heat. I feel comforted, sleepy. The moon was drawing me outside, into the night; now what is inside, the two of us together, the warmth of our bodies, has become more weighty; the darkening and brightening moon is far away.

How long have I slept? My mother, behind me, has turned away, is snoring. Before me the open window, the warm scented air drifting over us. The chinaberry tree, the mesquite, the honeysuckle, all are dripping in molten silver. The silence is vast and heavy, hangs like

ripe fruit. I roll over on my left side, lie against my
mother's back. Her nightgown has ridden up about her
waist; I feel the warmth, the firmness, the mass and
curves of her buttocks. I put my arm across her, my hand
coming to rest on her belly. My throat constricts. The
fingers venture lower, encounter the crinkly hair. I am
motionless, breathe slowly, deeply, through my mouth:
If she wakes she must find me asleep, must assume it by
chance that my hand found its way to this place. But she
is undisturbed, her gentle snoring regular. After a while
my fingers begin their prowl. I seek an entrance. The
skin from which this hair springs is firm, mounded,
spongy. Where is it? I move slowly from side to side,
from top to bottom, find nothing. An impenetrable wall.
I am shut out. Yet it *must* be here . . . somewhere. A
choked feeling in my throat, a strangled acrid taste. I wait
awhile, try again, feel my way back and forth through
every smallest part of this baffling triangle.

The snoring stops. I lie as if frozen. Minutes pass . . .
an eternity . . . the two of us motionless in an impenetra-
bly dense silence. Neither of us breathes. I should snore
to let her know that I am asleep, but am paralyzed. After
a while she sighs, extends her legs a bit, shifts her position. My inert hand is still in her tangle of hair. We have
come uncovered in this warm night. Minutes pass. Her
breathing becomes deep, she resumes her gentle snoring.
I relax. Behind my back the silver light comes and goes
as the high clouds pass before the moon, and directly
before me the moon of her behind gleams and disappears, gleams, winks, disappears.

She rolls over on her back. Under cover of her sleep I resume my stealthy search. Her legs have fallen somewhat apart—an opportunity lost to me because my only map for this primal quest is the drawings of naked women on toilet walls which portray an oval orifice fringed with hair in the lower abdominal wall. In that mysterious triangle back and forth my fingers go. An unbroken barrier. *It's not here!* My assault on a walled city is repulsed without even rousing the sleeping defenders. I withdraw my hand, impotent, humiliated, roll over on my right side facing the window. The moon regards me with an ironic stare, comes and goes with the dark clouds: "Here I am, now I'm gone! Catch me if you can!" A sour taste of defeat, of weakness, of rancor. I leave her, return to my cot on the back porch.

The next morning, getting dressed, hearing her move about in the kitchen, preparing breakfast, I think: If she is disapproving, she was awake; if not, she was asleep. As it turns out, she is unusually tender and loving with me throughout the day. But I am surly.

WHEN I WAS FOURTEEN my sister went away to college. My mother and I were now alone with each other. In the mornings she would get up first and prepare breakfast, which we would then eat together. She would leave for work the same time I left for school. She taught third grade, and I was a junior in high school. When we arrived back home in the afternoons she would often walk the mile or so to the grocery store. Returning, she would make beds, sweep, clean, wash, and prepare dinner. Afterward she would wash the dishes while I studied. When all the chores were done she would sit at the kitchen table with checkbook, budget, bills all spread out before her and "do the accounts," as she put it, which meant trying to figure out whether we could make it to the end of the month, and if not what expenses could be cut, or postponed. She had "no head for figures," as she said, so this was a tedious and inconclusive task, always to be continued the next night. Sitting at the table under the dim hanging light, she pondered, she moved her lips, repeatedly moistened the pencil on her tongue as if a hyperreadiness to write might make the bleak figures come out better, a deeply troubled expression on her face. If I showed concern she reassured me. "Oh, don't worry, son. We will find a way." Or, "It will all turn out for the best. God will look after us." But she didn't act as if she counted on help, from any source, but as if it were all up to her and she were failing.

About this time I gained a different image of her, came to see her life, not simply as she lived it day to day, but in extension. For six years she had enslaved herself to my father, a twenty-four-hour nursing duty, day after day. And the outcome of all those years of toil and devotion—he died, he was gone, and that wild piercing cry she flung after him, and no response, nothing. Where he had been was but a void.

She pulled herself together then, but only to begin a different kind of servitude: to her children. She had no special training or ability or experience, and no confidence in herself. She offered piano lessons, sold encyclopedias, finally got a job as study-hall teacher, went to night school and summer school, finally obtained a temporary teacher's certificate that had to be renewed each year by more courses. She was never sure we could make it. She knew we would not starve, for, at worst, we could move back to Louisiana and live with her parents and brothers; but it seemed important to her, for her children, that we have a home of our own. This was what she was struggling to achieve and to maintain. And was succeeding—but just barely.

It was about this time I came to see where her life was heading, and that she herself could neither see what lay ahead nor do anything about it. She enslaved herself to those who would leave her. June had already gone, and in two years I would be leaving—I could hardly wait. Then she would be alone. I worried about what would happen after I left.

I began to help her in ways that she would never have thought to ask. I took the list from her hand in the afternoons and walked to the store and came back with the groceries. I helped as she cooked our dinner. We washed the dishes together. I urged her to go out socially, to meet people. She was forty and I told her she should get married. She gratefully accepted my greater participation, and listened to my counsel with a kind of hungry bemusement. It meant a lot to her that I was talking to her, that I was urging something on her, that I was concerned, but the content of my urgings passed her by. I told her of specific social opportunities—a church picnic, a group of schoolteachers who met for square dancing, excursions to the Spanish missions. It was too late; these things seemed remote to her. What was real was that I needed new shoes and June needed an evening dress—and where would she find the money to send me to college? Where there should have been concern for self there was nothing.

Two more years pass and now I am sixteen and she is forty-two. I have graduated from high school, and, as she feared, there is no money to send me to college. So she writes to her brother, O.M., in Baton Rouge; and O.M. invites me to live with him and to attend Louisiana State University.

Now she is alone. She writes almost every day, and her letters are dull, dull, dull; for there's not much of interest to be extracted from her cramped routine. And I write to her several times each week because I don't want her to be disappointed. I know the pattern of her days, see her getting home about four in the afternoon after a long walk from school, tired and dusty, hasn't eaten, yet before entering the house she crosses the road to the row of mailboxes, and I feel how she will feel if the box is empty. And my letters to her are dull, dull, dull; for there's not much of interest to be extracted from dutifulness and guilt.

At Christmas I am home. She looks tired, thin. I ask about her eating. She brushes me aside. I persist and discover that she cooks very little. Mostly she eats scraps, whatever is at hand, often forgets. I scold her and lecture her; she thrives on my concern and promises to change. The spring semester passes, and I am again home for the summer. June graduates from college and gets a teaching job in Port Arthur, and in September I return to Baton Rouge.

Two weeks later my mother mentions being sick, has missed two days of school, but says she is already better. Her sister is coming to visit. Then nothing. I hear next from her sister, my Aunt Mit, who writes that she found my mother so weak she could not bear to leave her alone in San Antonio and so took her back with her to Comfort, Texas, where Mit's husband, Ike, is telegrapher on a spur line of the Southern Pacific. I continue to write encouragement and advice and continue to receive nondescript letters of vague optimism. In every letter she is "beginning to feel better." Then comes a letter from Mit saying that my mother is much worse; Mit is worried about having her there with her where no doctor is available, yet believes my mother to be too sick to be at home alone. Mit can't go with her to San Antonio and stay there with her, because she has a husband and two children of her own to look after.

I leave Baton Rouge the next day, changing in San Antonio to the freight train to Comfort, traveling in the caboose, which I have all to myself—except occasionally when the conductor climbs down from the roof to sit by the round coal-burning stove. The conductor lets me off at the switching station near Comfort. The tiny three-room house where my aunt and uncle live is no more than six feet from the tracks, yellow clapboard like all the company buildings along the Southern Pacific line. On the other side of the tracks is the tiny room where my uncle works as telegrapher. I enter the house. No one expects me. My aunt, astonished, takes me to my mother's room. I open the door, see her lying in bed, propped up on pillows. Her face is gaunt, the skin ashen, her white hair splayed out on the pillow, her eyes large and frightened. I see the shock of surprise sweep over her face, followed by a wave of doubt—perhaps she is hallucinating?—her mouth opens; the face contorts in anguish, hope, and disbelief.

"It's me, Mama. I've come to take you home."

In San Antonio I take her to see Dr. Whittaker, who looked after my father, who never charged us, and who now listens to her tale. She is nervous, her hands tremble, her limbs are weak, her gait unsteady, she has no appetite, has frequent hot flashes, and a peculiar rash on her arms and legs. Pellagra, he says, and prescribes a diet high in vitamin B with many leafy vegetables. She is too weak to be up, so I am the cook, and now do for her as she did for my father. I prepare the food, serve it to her in bed on a tray, urge her to eat, to force it if necessary; and she does. And then begins a diarrhea which eventually becomes bloody. Dr. Whittaker now puts her on a cereal diet; I prepare the brown mush three times a day. The diarrhea continues, the nervousness gets worse. Dr. Whittaker begins talking about a "hidden focus of infection," and goes looking: bladder, kidneys, tonsils. Finds nothing. He tries a drug for amoebic dysentery—just in case, he says. Nothing helps. Weeks pass, months. Winter with its rains. She cries a lot, she trembles, she can't stand without support. Every few weeks we go back to see Dr. Whittaker. He is at a loss, is casting about.

"There *must* be a hidden focus of infection," he says. And since everything else, he thinks, has been excluded, "It must be the teeth."

"My teeth don't hurt," my mother says. "That's maybe the one thing that seems all right."

"Nevertheless, it must be the teeth," he says. "To be safe I think we'd better have them out."

"All of them?"

"Yes."

My mother is shocked. At home she feels her teeth one by one with her fingers, tries to wiggle them; they are firm. "What should I do?" she cries. I do not know. I examine them myself. Her teeth are white and regular, I can't see anything wrong with them, but it has been explained to us that the infection may be at the roots and may never show. The only thing certain is that she is very sick and not getting better. We have no money with which to seek a second opinion, we do not know that this is urgently indicated, nor would we know where to seek it. "I don't know, Mama. I just don't know." We go to see Dr. Whittaker again: "In my opinion, Mrs. Wheelis, you should have these teeth removed." Her lips tremble; her forefinger resting on her worn purse makes frantic little waving movements. She acquiesces.

Now begins the grisly ordeal, four teeth a week. All are difficult extractions, usually with broken bone and broken roots. Each Friday morning we plod to the trolley, ride into the city. She emerges from the dentist's office, holding a bloody towel to her mouth. She can't speak. I comfort her on the trolley, tell her that though this is very hard and difficult now, maybe in time it will make her well. At the end of the line we get off; the motorman looks at us curiously. I hold her arm and support her around the waist as we slowly make our way on foot the mile to our house. She can't speak, is in an anguish of pain, of dismay at what is happening to her. In eight weeks all thrity-two teeth are removed. She is forty-four years old.

Now we must wait for healing before dentures can be fitted. I feed her liquids and puréed vegetables. Gradually she begins to feel better. We believe that the hidden focus of infection has been removed, that now perhaps she will recover. The diarrhea is not so bad, she can walk. She has gained some strength. An impression is made for her dentures. She begins to look forward to being able to chew again, to eat solid food. Eventually the great day arrives; we are to pick up the dentures at noon. I buy a steak, plan a celebratory meal, promise her a treat.

She looks puzzled as she emerges from the dentist's office. "Let me see," I say. She shakes her head. On the trolley she doesn't want to talk. "They feel strange," she says finally. "Let me see." She opens her mouth slightly. "They look fine," I tell her. She is nervous, unhappy. At home she lies on the bed, fans herself, is having hot flashes. I set the table, cut flowers in the yard, grill the steak. The festive meal is ready. She comes to the table.

Her hands tremble. I watch as she cuts the meat, lifts a small piece to her mouth. A tentative effort to chew, instantly aborted. Her face is still. The eyes fill with tears. She removes the meat from her mouth, begins to weep.

"I can't eat!" she wails. She rises from the table, flings herself through the house, onto the bed. I follow.

"It just takes time, Mama. You have to be patient. It will get better."

She sobs inconsolably.

ALL OF HER SYMPTOMS now get worse again: weakness, diarrhea, nervousness, hot flashes. The rash, however, has disappeared.

One night I wake to find her standing by my cot. "Son!"

"What is it, Mama?"

She trembles. "I'm frightened."

"What are you afraid of?"

"I don't know."

"Did you have a bad dream?"

"No. . . . I can't sleep." She shifts back and forth, one foot to the other. "Come lie with me for a while, son. Maybe that will help me."

I sit up on my cot, switch on the hanging light. She is shaking slightly, twisting her hands. I get up, put my arm around her. "Come on, Mama. I'll stay with you." I take her back to her room. She crawls into bed, holds open the covers for me. I sit on the edge of the bed, observe her disappointment. Again she holds up the covers for me to enter, a desperate entreaty on her face. I think of all those times when I was frightened and was made welcome to come into this bed. And I remember, too, that night when I was *not* frightened, but still was welcome, the night of the mysterious moon and the sailing clouds.

"I will do just about anything for you, Mama. But you mustn't ask me to come to bed with you." She lets the covers fall. "But I'll help you go to sleep." I turn off the light. "You're in your own bed now, and I'm right here beside you . . . looking after you . . . and nothing bad is going to happen. I'm going to stay right here with you. You've been hard sick . . . have gone through a bad time . . . but the worst is over and now you are beginning to get better." My tone is heavy, prophetic, incantatory. "Close your eyes now . . . because it is time for you to sleep. I'm going to stay right here with you. And I will tell you a story . . . and when I finish you will be asleep. And while you listen I want you to imagine something very heavy, a heavy stone perhaps. It is in your hands. Right now. You feel its heaviness . . . now. It's in your eyelids too. And I am telling you a story . . . about something that happened a long time ago . . . about a man who carried a stone just like the one in your hands . . . and felt all of its great heaviness . . . the same heaviness you feel now in your eyelids . . ."

GRADUALLY she improved. After a year she was able to be up and about. Her strength came back, but not completely. The illness had diminished her, left her weaker, more vulnerable. She was forty-five. Her hair was snow-white, her hands trembled, her eyes were very blue. She was well enough, I thought, for me to leave her, but not well enough for me to leave her alone. With difficulty I persuade her to put our house in the hands of a real-estate agent, and go back to Louisiana to live with her parents.

THE TWO OF US sit on a bench in the waiting room of the railroad station in San Antonio. My mother is wearing a black dress, shapeless and old. I sense in her a mounting agitation, and in myself a corresponding fear; I try to escape from both by pretending to read. The book in my hands is Kant's *Critique of Pure Reason*. She tries not to break in upon my apparent absorption.

At last, unable to keep still any longer, she asks, "What did we do with the living-room set?"

"Left it in the house," I murmur, without looking up from my book.

"Left it in the house?"

"You know that, Mother. We discussed it often enough," I say patiently.

"We shouldn't have left it," she says. "That's not the right kind of furniture to leave in a rented house. It's solid walnut. Your daddy bought it for me at an auction. We should have put it in storage."

The station vibrates slightly to an arriving train. I look at the clock and then across the waiting room to the bulletin board, where the incoming and outgoing trains are indicated in white chalk. There is still half an hour before the departure time of our trains, due to leave at almost the same moment, for different destinations. I try to go on reading, find that I can't concentrate, and close the book. My glance comes to rest first on my own luggage, a single suitcase, and then on my mother's four suitcases, two of them shabby and dilapidated, with heavy cord tied around them to keep them from bursting open.

"Don't you want me to check those two old suitcases?" I ask.

She does not appear to hear me. Her lips move, as if she is talking to herself.

"Mother," I say, touching her arm and then indicating the dilapidated suitcases. "I'd better check those two on your ticket."

"What's that?" she cries, her voice full of alarm. "What are you going to do?"

"I'm going to check your bags," I say, and stand up.

"No," she says. "Don't do that."

"You can't manage four by yourself," I say. "You have to change at Shreveport and Monroe. What if you can't find a redcap?"

"Hon," she says, brushing this problem aside, "where did we put that little baby dress of yours?"

I sigh and sit down. "I don't know. But it doesn't matter. It was falling apart anyway."

"Why, dear! I wouldn't part with that dress for the world. It's pure silk. Your grandmother spent months making it—before you were born. Didn't you see the fine handwork on it?"

"Yes," I say wearily. "I saw it. Don't worry. It must

be in one of the boxes we stored. It's bound to be there, because we didn't throw anything away. Nothing. Not even a thirty-year-old newspaper."

"I wish I could remember where my things are," she says plaintively.

Nervous and withdrawn, she sits and clutches her purse. A gray-haired Negro, red cap in hand, plants himself in front of the bulletin board and in a long, rolling cadence announces the arrival and impending departure of the Sunset Limited. Suddenly, Mama leans forward and unties the cord around one of the old suitcases. In spite of my protests, she opens the suitcase and begins going through the contents.

The bag is filled with fragments of the past, carefully folded and lovingly packed: surgical instruments that had belonged to my father; a souvenir of Lookout Mountain; a wedding veil; baby shoes; a bullet mold that was used by my great-grandfather; sheet music; bundles of ancient letters; a certificate of membership in the Woodmen of the World, dated 1905.

Many of these things I had previously thrown away as being of no value, and the rest I had put away for storage. She must have been up most of the preceding night retrieving and packing them.

Since she could never throw anything away, the closets and the attic had been piled high with old possessions, and the process of sorting and packing had brought to light innumerable items evocative of the past. Though ostensibly engaged in discarding the useless and packing the valuable, actually she had done neither. She had merely gone through our belongings one by one, fondled them, talked about them, and cried now and then. At the end of a morning's work, she would be surrounded by piles of souvenirs, from not one of which was she willing to be separated. I, on the other hand, had ransacked ruthlessly, and my mother had spent much of her time recovering the things I had thrown away. The work of one had neutralized that of the other. Sometimes we had both been in one of the large closets together, I on a stepladder plowing through a pile of miscellany on the top shelf. "We don't want this anymore," I would say, tossing something down on the floor. "Or this. Or this." And she, as these reminders of the past fell around her, would stoop and pick each one up, smooth it out, and place it lovingly among the things she wanted to keep.

"What in the world can you want with this?" I ask now as I lean over and take out a little brown bottle that I remember throwing in the trash several days before. She takes it from me. "Why, hon, this medicine once saved your life. You fell down a long flight of stone steps when you were just three years old. That was when we were up in Chattanooga, and your daddy said that if it hadn't been for this medicine, you would've died."

"What is it?" I ask.

"I don't know. I think it's adrenaline."

"Well, it's no good now!"

"I know, but I think we ought to keep it."

"What for?"

"Well, it saved your life," she says, putting the bottle

back in the suitcase. "We don't want to throw away any of our keepsakes."

She resumes her search, lifting sections of the contents of the suitcase here and there and peering in at the deeper layers. Presently, she says something under her breath and begins untying the other old suitcase. It is filled with a similar assortment of souvenirs. She looks through it, without finding what she is looking for. Then she sits up straight. "Hon, where did we put that picture of your daddy?"

"Which one?" I ask.

"The big one in the oval gold frame. You know—the one on the wall over the piano."

"We left it there."

"Left it there?" she repeats incredulously.

"You can have the agent mail it to you if you want it," I say.

For a moment she sits quite still. Then a stubborn expression comes over her face, and hurriedly she ties up the two suitcases. When she has finished, she gets up and walks away. I call to her. She stops, comes back, and picks up one of her suitcases. I go to her and take her arm. "Mama, what's the matter?" I ask. "What are you doing?"

"Well, now, son, sit down and I'll tell you," she says. "I'll tell you what I've decided." She pats my hand as we sit down on the bench. "I've decided I won't go."

"You *can't* change your mind now!" I cry. "Everything's all set. We're about to get on the train."

"No, I've made up my mind," she says. "This is my

home. All my things are here. I belong here."

"If *you* don't go, I can't go either," I say.

"Yes, you can, too. I wouldn't hold you back. It's right for you to go."

I look at the clock and swallow hard. "We've been through all this before," I say. "We've made the right decision. You've been very sick, and . . ."

"I know," she says, "and I'll never forget what you did for me. If you hadn't come home and looked after me, I'd not be living now. I'd . . ."

"That's not the point, Mama. Listen, please. Will you listen to what I say?"

"Yes, son."

"You're a lot better, but still not entirely well. You need a long rest. You know what the doctor told you. And I ought to go back to college."

"Yes, I know you should, hon."

"But the point is that you're not well enough to stay here alone."

"Why, yes, I am."

"There'd be no one to look after you if you got sick again. You wouldn't feed yourself properly."

"Yes, I will."

"You didn't the last time you were left alone."

"I've learned my lesson now."

"Mama, don't let's argue about it. It's all settled."

"But this is my home," she says. "What would I do in Marion?"

"Grandma and Grandpa are there," I say. "Uncle Kleber and Aunt Margaret are there. And Clayton. You can rest. You will have someone to talk to. And there'll be people to look after you."

"I don't need anyone to look after me."

"Yes, you do," I say. "I'm going to be away at school all winter, and probably all next summer. There's no sense in your staying here alone. You have no relatives near here. You'd be lonesome. You'd have to cook for just yourself, and keep up the house, and you wouldn't have anybody to talk to, or take care of you if you got sick. I just don't like to think of it."

"You and June will be coming home for your vacations," she says.

"It's not worth it, keeping the house just for that," I say.

"You mustn't worry about me, son. I've been looking after myself for a long time, and I certainly ought to know how by now."

I slump dejectedly. "All right, then," I say. "If you stay, I stay. I can't leave you alone."

"No, hon, that's . . ."

"I'm not going to discuss it any more," I say irritably. "I'm sick of it. We've been round and round this for weeks. Every time I think it's settled, you change your mind. Then we go through the same old thing all over again. I'm through talking about it. If you won't go, then I have to stay and look after you—at least until I can find someone else to do it."

A man sits down across the way, stares at us, begins to read a paper. I scuff the sole of one shoe against the other.

"All right, son," she says finally. "I'll go."

For several moments we sit in silence. Then she says, more to herself than to me, "I think I saw the photograph album just now. Where was it?" Again she unties one of the old suitcases.

"You really must let me check them," I say to her.

She finds the photograph album and for a few minutes seems relatively at peace as she turns its pages.

"Look, dear," she says, taking hold of my arm. "Do you know who that pretty little baby is?"

"No," I say, "but from the tone of your voice I gather it's me."

"Yes, it is," she says, and lapses into a sort of baby talk. "You were just the cutest, preciousest little baby there ever was. That's what you were!"

Gently disentangling myself from her grasp, I say, "You'd better let me close up this bag now." When I have retied the suitcase, I find her looking at a small, faded tintype. "Who's that?" I ask.

"Your daddy as a boy. See the date on it? It was taken in Monroe, in 1893."

She began to cry. "How can I go?" she asks. "All my things are in my house. There's no other place to put them. Nobody else will ever take care of them—you know that. It'll never be the same after other people live there. They'll bang things up, be careless and destructful of the things we love!"

People are looking at her curiously. I am embarrassed.

"Don't feel so bad about it, Mama," I say in a low voice, putting my arm around her. "Of course there'll be some wear and tear, but you'll be getting rent. Maybe when you come back, you'll have enough money saved to fix the house up like you've been wanting. Anyway, we're not leaving anything that's valuable."

The words have little meaning for her, but she drinks in the kindness and seems comforted.

"I don't know what I'd do without you, dear," she says. "You're always so good to me."

"You'll be all right."

"I know I will," she says.

"Now, try to relax, Mama. It's almost train time. Don't look through the bags anymore. Nothing has been lost."

"All right, dear." She folds her hands in her lap, as if making an effort to compose herself. Once, she leans forward to do something with one of the suitcases, but catches herself and sits up straight again. "You know, hon," she says presently, "we won't go on to Marion tonight. We're both tired. When we get to Shreveport, we'll go to a hotel and get a good night's sleep."

I feel a cold hand at my heart. "Mother! You know, don't you, that I'm not going with you?"

"Where are you going?" she asks.

"Mother! Pull yourself together, *please!* I'm going to Baton Rouge—to school. You know that."

"Oh, yes—yes."

I look away and take a deep breath, feel a mounting anxiety. I look at the clock. Another fifteen minutes. I have an intense longing to have it over.

She takes one of my hands in hers. "I wish you could go to Marion with me," she says. "After all, you need a vacation, too."

I extract my hand. "Are you sure you won't let me check two of your bags?" I ask. "It'd be a lot easier for you."

"You do whatever you think best, dear."

"I have to have your ticket," I say.

She gives it to me, and I pick up the two old bags. She holds my arm and looks at me as though she will not allow me out of sight. "I'll go with you," she says.

"No, Mother, please! You stay here with our other things. I'll be right back."

Reluctantly she sits down. I feel her eyes following me as I cross the station. After checking the bags, I stand around the baggage room for a few minutes.

"You know," she says as soon as I return, "I've been thinking—and I've got an idea that seems very good to me."

"What is it?"

"Why don't I go to Baton Rouge with you . . . ? Instead of to Marion? We could rent an apartment with what we get from our house here. We'd be together and could look after each other. I could make a home for you. I'd like that."

"I don't think that's a good idea, Mother."

"Why not, hon?"

"Things are too uncertain. I don't want you to have

to do housework and shopping and cooking. You need a long rest. There are a lot of reasons."

"We could make out all right if we were together," she says.

"No, I don't think it would be wise."

"Don't you want me with you?"

"Of course, Mother. I'm just telling you what I think best for both of us."

"I know you are," she says quickly.

"Come on, Mama," I say, unable to wait any longer. "I think I heard them announce your train. Anyway . . . we can get on now."

I pick up the three remaining bags, and we go down into the underpass and come up at Track 5, where her train is standing. The conductor waits beside the steps of the first coach. He stands aside for us to board the train. She hesitates. I put my own suitcase on the platform and gently impel her forward by pressure on her arm, but she holds back.

"Go ahead, Mother."

She turns and catches the lapels of my coat, as though afraid of the train.

"Go ahead," I tell her. "I'll get on with you."

This magically overcomes her reluctance, and she climbs the steps. When we are seated on facing green plush seats, she leans forward with a worried expression, as if she can no longer put off telling me something of the greatest importance; yet she says nothing. Unable to avoid her eyes indefinitely, I force myself to look at her, and smile. She catches my hand in both of hers, presses it, caresses it, pleading mutely that I not go entirely away from her, that I save some part of my life and heart for her.

"Well," I say, "I guess it's about time to go."

She looks at me with eyes large and wet with tears. "Be a good boy, son," she says. "I know you will. Get plenty of sleep and don't work too hard."

As she obviously has not finished, I wait, but she seems lost in thoughts of a different nature and does not continue.

The car is filling up. A woman with a baby sits down across the aisle from us. The baby is crying. A porter squeezes by our seats, carrying four handbags. A newsboy comes down the aisle hawking the *San Antonio Express,* and makes two sales.

"I really have to go now," I say. "This train is going to leave in a minute, and mine is, too. Well—good-by, Mama."

I put my arms around her. Suddenly the thought of losing me seems to strike her with new force; she holds on to me and will not let go. I look down on the white hair and feel agonizingly small. I loosen her arms gently and turn away. After a few steps down the aisle, I stop and call to her. "Have you got your ticket?"

She is looking at me and does not understand. "What? What's that?"

"Your ticket?" I say.

"My ticket?"

The expression of annoyance that sweeps over my face seems to make her comprehend. "Oh," she says. "Oh, yes. You gave it back to me."

For a moment more, my glance meets hers. I try to smile affectionately; then I turn and quickly leave the car.

Passing her window on the outside, with my suitcase, I look up and see her eyes anxiously fixed on me through the glass. I smile, wave, and go on. After about twenty feet, I stop again, look back, and find that she has turned around in her seat, so as to follow me with her eyes until the last possible moment. I throw her a kiss. She returns the gesture with clumsy haste, dropping her purse as she does so.

I descend the steps to the underpass, come up again at Track 6, and board the train that will take me to Houston, Lake Charles, and on to Baton Rouge. When I am seated, I glance out the window and, to my surprise, find that I can still see my mother. Our trains are on adjacent tracks, and a distance of only a few feet separates the car I am sitting in from hers. I see her clearly and, were it not for the layers of glass, could speak to her. She is still looking backward, in the direction in which I had gone. Her hands grip her purse tightly. She is wearing the old black dress that has been her Sunday best for so many years. When she turns and settles in her seat, I think surely she will see me. But almost immediately she looks back again, as if on the remote chance that I might reappear.

My train leaves first. As it begins slowly to move, it

must have created for her the illusion that her train was moving—for she looks back more urgently, twisting her body, straining for one more glimpse of me. In this attitude of yearning, loss, and farewell, she disappears from my view.

The
Architect

The pigeon was interfering with his work, his livelihood. The vendor got angry. Why do you make such a thing of it?

Because . . . if he had whacked off the head . . . in anger . . . sure. I could accept that. But the feet.

Head, feet, one pigeon more or less? What's the big deal?

There's a lot in life that can only be mourned; there are some few things that must be hated.

FROM 1934 TILL 1953 my mother lived in Marion, Louisiana, in the big house where she was born—turrets and tower rooms and lightning rods, curving verandas, filigree gingerbread, porch swings, and a vast yard with

massive oak trees and towering sweet gum trees, all surrounded by a white picket fence. Her father, Oliver
Hazard Thompson, had built this house in 1887. As a
young country doctor in Alabama he had developed tuberculosis, and had been given three bits of advice by his
father: to go west, to drink plenty of whiskey, and to stay
out in the open air. He did all three. He left Alabama on
horseback, rode into northern Louisiana, and settled in
Union Parish. He built a store and an office in a clearing
of trees on the red clay soil; a few years later he built a
Methodist church for the circuit rider, and over the years
the village of Marion formed itself around him. For
many years he was the only doctor within a day's journey. He delivered babies, pulled teeth, sutured wounds,
set broken bones. His medicines were morphine, digi-
talis, calomel, castor oil, and quinine. When someone
came to get him he closed the store and set out on horseback. As he got older and the roads were better, he rode
in a buggy. He wore high-top black shoes and a shiny
black suit. A gold watch chain was always threaded
across his vest. He had a full black beard that gradually
turned gray. He always addressed his wife, Molly, as
"Mrs. Thompson" ("Pass the biscuits, Mrs. Thompson!"), and my mother, his firstborn, as "Daughter." He
built his big house about a hundred yards from the store,
and when dinner, as the noon meal was called, was
ready, Molly would stand on the porch and ring the bell,
and everyone in town would know that the doctor was
closing the store and going home for dinner. He had
nine children, of whom three died in infancy. Four boys

and two girls survived. The oldest boy, Kleber, came back to Marion after college and took over the store. The youngest son, Clayton, never left home.

When Oliver grew too old to practice medicine he still went every day to his office in the store, sat behind the dusty rolltop desk with the skull and the scales and the microscope, and talked with customers and visitors. He became in time a nuisance for Kleber, who wanted him out of the way. "You've lived long enough, Papa," Kleber would say. "It's time for you to die." Oliver would view him warily: "I'm better acquainted around here, son, than I will be anyplace I'm likely to go. So I reckon I'll just stay awhile longer."

In 1935 Molly died, and a year later Oliver. My mother stayed on then with her brother Kleber and his wife, Margaret, and their two girls, Patsy and Mary Grace, and her youngest brother, Clayton. On Sunday mornings she taught Sunday school and stayed for the sermon at the Methodist church, Tuesday evenings she went to choir practice, Wednesdays to prayer meeting, and every morning she walked up the red clay road to the school on the hill where she taught third grade. I visited her in Marion once or twice a year; and, whenever invited, she would visit me—in New York or Topeka or Stockbridge, Massachusetts.

IN 1946, back from the war in the Pacific, I had just begun psychiatric training at the Menninger Clinic when my mother again fell sick. After a few weeks her brother, my Uncle Kleber, telephoned from Marion to say that she was now hospitalized in Monroe. When I spoke to her physician on the phone he could tell me nothing except that she was seriously ill, diarrhea again the main symptom; perhaps a salmonella infection. Nothing could be cultured from her blood or her stools. When I arrived at her bedside I found her extremely weak. She was running a fever of 102 to 103 and had developed phlebitis of the left leg. Her hemoglobin was low, presumably because of the continuing bowel hemorrhage. "It's a nonspecific ulcerative colitis," her doctor said. "There's nothing to be done but bedrest." I discharged the doctor, transferred her to another hospital, and found a good internist.

I lay on a stretcher beside her bed as blood was taken from my vein and dripped into hers. She improved a bit. All lab tests were still negative. I thought she had an intestinal parasite and undertook to look for it, still close enough to my medical school days, I hoped, to recognize something like an amoeba. I spent hours in the hospital lab examining stool specimens under the microscope. And found nothing. And was about to give up when one day, searching among the myriad of vegetable cells which characterized every slide, it occurred to me that these were not vegetable cells at all but *Balantidium coli,* a large protozoan. And a pathogen. I had been seeing these cells for days without recognizing what they were. I rushed to the atlas of parasites to verify my discovery; the internist and the lab director soon confirmed it. It was a runaway case of balantidiasis. She was started immediately on Carbarsone. Her temperature dropped to normal on the second day; her appetite returned, she was able to eat; and by the fourth day the diarrhea and bleeding were over.

This experience completed her apotheosis of me. "If you had been my doctor thirteen years ago," she said, "I'd still have my teeth." To anyone who would listen she extolled my virtues, my accomplishments, and as she grew older her praise became excessive, eventually fatuous. "He saved my life. Not just once . . . twice! I would not be here today except for him. He is a supreme diagnostician! You can *mark that down!* The doctors had all given up. They didn't know what to do. They could *not* make a diagnosis. They didn't know what medicine to give me. Then *he* came. He was engaged in very important work in Topeka, Kansas. In *psychiatric* work. At the Menninger Clinic. But he dropped everything. He laid it all aside and came to see about me. And when he arrived . . . well, that's when everything changed. He got me the best doctor, and put me in the best hospital. He gave me two pints of his own blood. That's what *really* cured me! And then he made a diagnosis. Nobody else could do it. They all tried. They couldn't do it. He looked through the microscope, and kept looking, and kept looking, until he discovered the cause. And then he knew what would cure it. Carbarsone."

In her family, in childhood, she had learned that men bear the weight of the world; women are helpmeets. Only men may hold authority, deserve admiration; women tend to be foolish, weak, and easily frightened. Now she pushed this invidious stance to a further extreme, disparaged her own intelligence the further to exalt mine. "Let me tell you . . . what was wrong with me . . . it was so rare, so difficult to diagnose . . . that I can't even pronounce it. What is it, Allen? Balytodisus? Baly-ti-dai-pus? You see! I can't even say it."

Her recovery was not, however, complete. The phlebitis left her with a permanently swollen foot and leg. The ankle had disappeared; the leg was now of uniform size from calf to foot. A special shoe was required. She walked with a shuffle. Over the years, whenever she came to visit, she would ask me to go shopping with her for elastic hose. And always I would go, but in vain. The hose that she was able to pull on did not provide enough support, while the hose that did provide enough support was impossible for her, with her fumbling ways, to pull on over the swollen foot.

WHENEVER SHE VISITS US , a change comes over my wife. Normally gentle and rather quiet, she becomes abrupt, almost curt. A reaction, she says, to my mother's overly fond behavior with me. I understand; I, too, am often embarrassed by my mother's need to be near me, to touch me. When, before retiring, I go into the kitchen for a snack, my mother will always follow. "Can I get you some milk?" she will say, though the answer is always no. And always she will kiss me good night, holding me a few moments longer than I would wish. In the evenings after supper the three of us sit out on the front porch. When night comes my wife will go in to put the children to bed, and then my mother will begin to reminisce, her voice taking on a tone of clandestine warmth and intimacy. When I, too, wish to go in she will lean toward me in the darkness and take my hand and say, "Don't leave me, son, not yet."

WHEN IT CAME TIME for her to retire she wanted to leave Marion, to settle down near one of her children. Where should that be? She wanted to be near me, but I advised otherwise. I would probably be leaving Stockbridge soon, I told her, I didn't know when or where, and then would doubtless move still again. She should not tie herself to my uncertainties.

My advice was like an order. Disappointed but obedient, she turned to my sister, bought a little house in Midland, Texas, one block from June.

But was not happy. She did not complain to me, but complained a lot to June. To me she was respectful, admiring, deferential, tactful; to her daughter she was dissatisfied, demanding, often scornful, sometimes contemptuous. June had married "beneath her station"; Francis, her husband, "lacked breeding and culture," he had "no refinement, no education"; both were subjected to relentless comparisons with me. She was constantly telling my sister what to do, what to stop doing, how to live her life.

And Francis himself was demeaning of June, putting her down, spraying her with sarcastic cracks. Caught between the two of them, my sister began to falter. She was able to survive only by virtue of her work; for she was a much-loved schoolteacher, becoming eventually superintendent of schools, and this vocational success was ballast against the buffetings at home. But when forced by age to retire she was rendered helpless. Francis too was now retired, could devote himself full-time to the put-down of his wife; and my sister, subject now to hammer blows from both quarters, began to fall apart.

INCREASINGLY IT seemed to me that I was the architect of my mother's life, and as the years passed—straining and adventurous for me, gray and impoverished for her, years of waiting, always waiting for my rare and brief visits—it seemed that I unintentionally had designed for her a barren life, and that she was obediently following my blueprint, unable to break away from my spell, and I powerless to free her.

So perhaps my dying father was right to fear that she would fall for the first man to lay hand on her flank, but he could hardly have known that that man would be I, that therefore the promise not to remarry which he extracted from her could not protect her.

The
Little
Boy

Why are you haunted by that pigeon without feet? That Flying Dutchman of the air?

I was there. I looked into those twinkling eyes. I have been made custodian.

Is not the pigeon an odious bird? Are we not blessed when there is one less? However dispatched?

No. Not "however."

But do you not know about life? The way things are? That the great men of history are great because of sending others to die? Their greatness proportional to the numbers slaughtered?

I do not accept the way things are. I abhor great men.

Then why not mourn something worthy? At the Falaise Gap the Germans fell so thickly that, afterwards, for hundreds of yards you stepped on bodies, on limbs, viscera, heads—all of them sons and lovers, all webbed in hope, drenched, each one of them, in memory and desire. At Tarawa the U.S. Marines clawed their way ashore on and over and through their dying comrades, amid their screams, their hands so bloody they could not hold their rifles. At Belsen the naked Jews, white and stiff in death, bounce like firewood as they are thrown up on the roof-high stacks. And you—*you* are upset about a pigeon?

No act of cruelty must go undespised.

Was not that vendor a man like any other? Is there not cruelty in all of us? Did not that vendor go home, like the rest of us, and dandle his granddaughter on his knee, comfort her when she stubbed her toe?

He may dandle her on his knee till hell freezes over and still I'll hate him for what he did to that bird. I will never forget, will never forgive.

A FEW DAYS after my mother comes to visit, usually as we sit at dinner, she turns to me. "Son . . ." she says, her tone and manner announcing something portentous, "son, I'd like for you to show me your office." As if she had never seen it before—though in fact she sees it every time. And a day or two later, "Don't forget . . . I'd like you to show me your office." Not that she wants to *see* it; she wants *me* to *show* it to her. "All right," I say, "let's do it right now." We squeeze into the tiny elevator, descend, I open the double doors, we enter my private realm. Teak parquet floor, teak-paneled walls, rosewood bookshelves to the ceiling, oriental rugs. A deep silence inhabits this room. It embraces her, enfolds her. She smiles, begins a slow tour, touches the spines of books, feeling a vast awe at what I have read, examines the pictures, is contentedly bewildered at the Expressionist prints, content because their incomprehensibility to her is tribute to my sophistication and acumen; examines the couch. "Do your patients lie here?" "Some of them." She lies down. "And they talk?" "Yes." She sits before me in the large chair of brown leather.

"What do you *need?*" she says. She wants to make something for me to use in this room. A pillow for my couch perhaps; she has saved some pretty silk scraps, could put together a very nice pillow for me, she'd love to do it. Or perhaps a lap robe for my legs on cold days; she would crochet it in dark blue mohair. Or something else. Anything.

I sit directly before her in my own massive black leather chair. In silence we confront each other—son to mother, psychoanalyst to patient, Oedipus to Jocasta. She strokes the soft leather, caresses it. "Your patient sits here?" "Yes." "Where I am sitting?" "Yes." "And you sit there . . . where you're sitting?" "Yes." "And she . . . your patient . . . talks about herself—is that right?" "Yes." "And tells you all her troubles?" "Yes." "And you tell her what to do?" "Well . . . not exactly." She falls silent; a look of vast longing spreads over her face. *She* wants to be my patient, wants to come every day, and not just for fifty minutes, but for a session without end, wants to tell me her troubles, all she longs for.

But she does not permit herself to say these things. Watching her face, I see the exact moment her thoughts veer away from unutterable longing to a less anguished realm. "So she sits here and talks . . . and you sit there and listen? . . . Is that right?" "Yes." She clicks her tongue slightly. "Son . . ." She lowers her voice, and something of incredulity, perhaps of faint reproach, and yet of pride, enters her voice; perhaps she remembers the life of her husband, my father, as a country doctor. "Son . . . you have a *mighty* easy profession."

AND ONE MORE TIME, often on the eve of her departure, she will say, "I'd like to see your office once more . . . before I go." And again we fit ourselves into the tiny elevator and descend, and again she walks around my room, touching things, looking, thinking. In the upper rooms of this house I belong to my family, and she is a visitor; but here I belong to no one. This is the realm of my private self. Here she encounters only me—me, for whom she is searching. She thinks of what she might make for me that I would use in this room. She wants to create something with her own hands, with love, that will stay here with me, always, her surrogate, always with me.

IN 1970, when she was eighty-one years old, a mass appeared in her right breast. Over the phone the surgeon said it was cancer, recommended radical resection. I demurred, decided on a simple mastectomy if it were confirmed as malignant.

When I arrived in Midland she was so happy to see me that she forgot about the operation. When reminded of it, she wanted me to examine her.

"That's not necessary, Mama."

"But I *want* you to feel it."

"No matter what I might find," I said, "you would still have to have the biopsy."

"I know, I know, but I want you to feel it."

"If it *is* cancer, Mother, we're concerned that it not spread. So the less manipulation the better."

"You're my doctor," she said. "Your hands couldn't hurt me."

She took off her blouse, took off her bra, stood directly before me. "Lift your arms," I said. I could see a slight puckering of skin in the upper outer quadrant of the right breast. When I took the breast in my hands, I found the mass to be about the size of a golf ball, irregular in shape, very hard.

"The biopsy will be done while you're anesthetized," I told her. "You must be prepared for the possibility that when you wake, your breast will have been removed."

"I'm prepared," she said. "I'll do whatever you say."

So the breast was amputated. There were no metastases. She recovered quickly.

"I'm still your mother," she said—proudly, defiantly—"even with one breast!"

WHENEVER I INVITE HER to visit, she instantly and happily accepts. She comes several times each year, stays two or three weeks each time. After ten days or so I will see a worried expression, she will touch my arm, say, "Well . . ." very tentatively, "I guess we should think about my getting back home." A bleak little trial balloon; she's hoping I will shoot it down. And I do: "It's too early to think about that. You've just got here." "Well . . ." The tension drains away, she sighs, a contented look comes to her face, perhaps even something of smugness, of possession.

She is outspoken and fulsome in her praise of my wife, but the ulterior aim behind these ostensibly spontaneous outpourings, hidden from her, is painfully visible to the psychoanalysts whom she so disingenuously addresses. My wife becomes irritable, I become uncomfortable.

After a few more days, "Well . . . I guess I should begin packing up now," she says. "I guess I've had my visit out." "Why don't you stay another week?" I say. "Well, son . . . if you're sure I won't be in the way." "You're not in the way at all." She seems content with these negotiations, perhaps even feels herself to have been deviously successful.

And now she has seven more days to be with me—a lifetime! Anything can happen in seven days.

But then the seven days are gone, and we are at the airport, the loss imminent and unavoidable, and what then is urgently present in her tremulous voice and gait, the tension in her fingers on my arm, the desperate searching in her eyes, is that she wants to stay with me forever, that no *visit* could ever be long enough, that any separation is a death.

DURING HER eighties my mother's upper spine slowly collapsed, diminishing her height by about six inches. Her esophagus, now much too long for the shortened distance from her throat to her stomach, formed kinks, and the swallowing of solid food became difficult. Several times a morsel of something like steak would fail to pass, would lodge there, halfway down, creating in her a helpless choked discomfort. Sometimes it would take days to pass. I was constantly urging her to take small bites, to chew thoroughly, to drink water as she ate.

A huge hump formed on her back. At ninety she was deeply stooped over, walked with a cane in small, slow, shuffling steps, and what presented forward as she came toward me was not her face but the crown of her head. Her face stared at the ground; she had begun her final plunge into the earth. When she heard my voice and saw my feet before her she would reach out and climb my arms with her hands, thereby managing to lift her face enough to see me.

WHEN SHE WAS eighty-three it became evident that she could not continue to live alone. She was doddering and indecisive in street intersections, got lost on the way to the grocery store. She would put something on the stove and forget it until the house filled with smoke. She could no longer walk to church or to prayer meetings, could not visit friends, was increasingly isolated. I urged her to enter Trinity Towers, a nearby retirement home where several of her friends now lived. "Meals will be prepared for you," I told her, "and it will be easy for you to find companionship." She was reluctant. "I will keep your house intact," I promised her, "just as it is. You can move back anytime you like. Only if *you* decide to stay there permanently, only then will we sell this house."

At ninety she became incontinent of urine and had to be diapered, needed assistance in dressing and undressing and in bathing; so I moved her from Trinity Towers to Spring Park, a nursing home. She was no longer steady enough to walk with a cane; she got about the hallways slowly in a walker. In the short distance from her room to the dining room she would lose her way.

ALWAYS I DELAY calling my mother—because it is so hard to get off the phone. One thing reminds her of another; the chain of reminiscence is endless, ranges not only over her own long life, but gathers in friends and relatives, extends back into what her grandmother told her about her great-great-grandmother. After five or ten minutes I begin trying to say good-by: "It's time for me to stop. I must help with dinner now." Whereupon she tells me what she has had for dinner, and the wonderful dinners her mother used to prepare, the vegetable garden when she was a child, and Mamie the black cook, and the time when her sister, Mit, left the arsenic in the pantry and everybody got sick and they all thought it was Lit the handyman who had done it. "Now I really have to stop, Mother," I say. "There are things I have to do before . . ." "Yes, I know," she says, "and I mustn't keep you, but before we say good-by I want to tell you that . . ." and off into another story.

That's the way it was until her ninety-seventh year when, one day, I realized with surprise that I had called her during my ten-minute break between patients, that I had fallen into the habit of calling at such times, and that it was easy to get off the phone. The stickiness was gone. Her densely peopled past had, like old film, faded to uniform gray.

When I go to visit her in the nursing home I try to bring it back. "Do you remember our house in San Antonio?" She looks puzzled, then troubled, "No . . . I can't say I do . . . not exactly, no." I then describe it for her, the kitchen, the long veranda, the hackberry tree, the mesquite, the honeysuckle that covered the fence, the cot on the back porch where I slept. As I talk I see in her face glimmers of recognition; I step up my pace, try to compact those glimmers into a chain reaction of re-call. Everything is lost. I ask about her marriage. Nothing. Her years in college? Nothing. I remind her of the time when her father took her as a little girl on a river-boat to New Orleans, where, having bought an entire bunch of bananas, he locked her in the hotel room so she would be safe while he went off to play poker. The high point of her childhood. I've heard it a hundred times. Don't you remember? Nothing. She peers back into a void.

YOUNG BLACK WOMEN, enormous, slow-moving, strong, lift her off the bed into the wheelchair, onto the toilet, wipe her behind, bathe her, dry her, hold her up, dress her. She watches, helpless, troubled, as they ransack her drawers; things once carefully folded tumble about under heedless, uncaring hands as they search for underwear, nightgowns, hairbrush, dentures, blouses. She does not trust these women. She hides the candy I bring her in bottom drawers, inside vases, behind photographs.

She has misplaced her pearls. I search her handbags, her desk, her closet. Going through the pockets of her clothes, I come upon a piece of dry cake wrapped in Kleenex, half an apple, gray with age. Under a pile of stockings I find a carefully wrapped sandwich. "That's for the little boy," she says. But no pearls.

As SHE LOST the past, she lost also the present. Vision blurred and dimmed; she could not read or write, could not make out what was happening on the television screen. Books and newspapers fell away. She no longer hears the telephone: I must call the nurses' station, ask that someone go to her room and pick it up for her. No more does she shuffle down the hallway in a walker; she lives in a wheelchair.

Emptied of past, bereft of present, without future, she begins to create an imaginary world. "The little boy has been hanging around today," she says. "I think he wants to talk to me, but he won't come close. I'm gonna get some candy; he'll like that." Over the months this little boy becomes a companion, a fixture in her life. She worries about him. Where are his parents? They should be looking after him. A little boy like that needs a home. He should not be out alone at night. She would take him in herself if she could, but it's hard for her to get about. Always she tries to feed him. In the dining room she asks the waitress to set a place for him. "Ain't no little boy here, Miz Wheelis," the waitress says. Whereupon my mother becomes cross, demands an additional plate, and, not getting it, puts aside some of her own food and takes it back to her room.

SHE LOOKS AT her hands. Ancient, withered, discolored, gnarled with arthritis, leaping veins and tendons. A plain wedding band on her fourth finger, a large amethyst in gold setting on her middle finger. She touches them, hesitates, moves them back and forth, finally takes them off. "Look at them," she says. Her manner is portentous. Inside the wedding band: OMT and ABW, June 19, 1908. "I want you to take them with you . . . to keep them safe." I protest: She enjoys them, she should keep them. "No. I'll lose them. You take care of them for me. Keep them safe. I want Joan to have them . . . someday." I drop them into my pocket. Her eyes follow their disappearance, linger on the pocket.

TIED TO THEIR WHEELCHAIRS like rag dolls, sticklike shanks and arms, arthritic joints, backs twisted and humped, spindly necks, palsied hands and heads, vacant stares; some with napkins around their necks being fed by young black women, "C'mon, honey . . . open your mouth . . . swallow it down . . . there's a good girl," food dribbling from their chins; some feeding themselves, dropping soup down their blouses, chasing peas blindly around their plates with tremulous hands; some slumped forward head on knees, oblivious of food, of everything. Over the Muzak a muted rock and roll. The young serving women talk of dates and dresses as they shove food at withered, resisting mouths. A woman with fixed stare croaks, "Silent night . . . holy night . . . all is calm . . . all is bright." Another pounds the table in a slow insistent rhythm chanting, "Tah!-rah!-rah!-boom!-by!-yay!" My mother, hearing nearly gone, hears this, lifts a finger: "The little boy is singing. He is singing your name." A woman with white hair flying wildly recites in a child's falsetto:

> "Jesus loves me, this I know,
> For the Bible tells me so.
> Little ones to Him belong;
> We are weak but He is strong."

On my next visit, as we sit talking, she seems to be waiting for something. "Where are my rings?" she says. "In San Francisco, Mother. Don't you remember? You wanted me to look after them for you . . . so they wouldn't get lost." "Yes . . . but I could wear them while you're here. They'd be safe as long as you're with me." "Well, that's true," I say, "and I'm sorry I didn't think of it myself. Next time I'll bring them."

A few months later I'm back, and give her the rings.

She receives them eagerly, hungrily; with something like a sigh, a visible relaxation, she slips them on her fingers, she is whole again. During the next two days I watch her affirm herself in these rings. They contain the past that is lost to her. When it is time for me to go she again, reluctantly, surrenders them. "No, Mother, I'm not going to take them. They would simply lie in my desk. Useless. But you really enjoy them. I want you to have them. I want you to wear them all the time."

THE VISIT is over. "Good-by, Mama."

She fixes me with a look of solemn entreaty. "Son . . ." she takes my hand, presses it between both her own. "Son . . . why don't you take me back with you? . . . I wouldn't be much trouble and I could help with the chores."

I look at the sagging eyelids, the clouded, unseeing eyes. Incontinent, diapered, having to be lifted onto the toilet, into bed, unable to feed herself, strapped in the chair that she not pitch forward. "I'd like to, Mama . . . but you're too weak to make the trip. You have to get back some strength first. Then I'll take you."

She looks at me dubiously, takes a grain of hope, but not more. It flickers briefly and fades. She stares at the wall, then turns to me in desperate resolve. "Well, I can tell you one thing," she says emphatically, "if you ever get down bad sick and have to be hospitalized . . . then I'm gonna come out there and look after you. I'm gonna come . . . even if I have to walk every step of the way. I'm gonna see to it that you get the *proper* medical care, and the *proper* food to help you get strong . . . and then I'm gonna stay awhile."

ONE DAY , having neglected her for a while, I call the nurse to get my mother on the line. There comes the thin, vacant voice, changing to warm as she recognizes me. She wants to talk but has nothing to say. I chat, I tell her news of my children. She doesn't remember them. I describe them to her, relate her experiences with them, try to make them come back. Nothing. She does not remember that I live in California or she in Texas, does not know what month it is, what year. She reproaches herself for having neglected her parents recently: I tell her they have been dead for fifty years, and that she was a great comfort to them in their last illnesses. She is reassured. And when am I coming to see her? She thinks I am just around the corner, cannot imagine me two thousand miles away.

"And how is the little boy?" I ask. "Oh, he's all right . . . I reckon." "Do you talk to him?" "Oh yes, I talk to him." "And does he answer you?" "He shies away. Don't seem to want much to do with me." "What's his name?" I have never asked this before. "Why his name is . . . Allen . . ." A slow wonderment spreads out in her voice. ". . . Wheelis. . . ." A slight startle of breath, a double take. "Funny . . ." She hesitates. "He has the same name as you!" Silence. I wait. Will she discover significance here or only coincidence? The moment drags, passes. Nothing. My childhood is lost to her. "Sometimes I won't see him for quite a spell," she says, "but then one day I'll hear a blood-curdling yell. . . ." She chuckles. "And then I'll know he's around."

That cry leaps from a deep well, without context or connection. She has no idea what it means, nor why she feels comfort rather than alarm. But I know. I remember that cry and the fantastic power it claimed.

AT TWELVE I discovered Tarzan and fashioned an identity on the life of this dauntless and unvanquishable savage. I would live in the jungle as he did, would survive on but my own strength and ingenuity, would be protector of all the friendly animals and the terror of the evil ones. I took Tarzan as my middle name. The trees roundabout were carved with the letters ATW. I wanted to depart civilization at once but knew I was too young. I had to wait . . . to prepare myself. But how long? Until sixteen, I decided. Then I would be ready. But would my mother let me go? I must get her promise.

I held close the details, said only that I wanted to live in Africa. "But at sixteen? . . . No. You have to go to college." "Please, Mama." "We don't have to decide now," she suggested. "You're only twelve." "Please, Mama. It's terribly important to me. Promise." "I can't promise such a thing, son. It might not be right for you. Let's wait." "I can't wait, Mama. I have to know now. *Please!*" She is silent, troubled. "A lot can happen between now and then," I add deviously, encouraging her to believe that I will change my mind about wanting to do such a thing, that therefore she will never have to deliver on this promise; while knowing that I will hold her to it even though I, in bad faith, seduced her into making it. "Just say yes. Please, Mama!" She sighs. "All right, hon."

The way is clear, the fantasy unrolls. At sixteen I will hitchhike to Galveston, will get a job on a freighter. Eventually this freighter will touch at Casablanca, where I will jump ship, find work on a coastal steamer going south. At the mouth of the Congo I'll pick up a riverboat, go upstream, deep into the interior. The river narrows. One night I will silently let myself over the side into the dark water, swim to the shore, disappear into the trackless jungle.

I viewed the next four years as preparation. I must become strong, must acquire the basic skills of survival. I raced down the veranda, leapt to the mesquite tree, swung about on the branches. I practiced climbing with ropes, threw spears, made flint knives. And frequently, after mortal combat, I rehearsed that celebrated moment of epiphany: Placing my right foot on the body of vanquished foe, I threw back my head, beat upon my chest, and uttered the victory cry of the bull ape. I had never heard such a cry, nor was I, in Texas, likely to. Knowing only that on hearing it all the "denizens of the jungle" trembled, I improvised the loudest, most prolonged and alarming cry I could imagine, then practiced to make it uniform, distinctive, and terrifying.

And one afternoon, lost in my reverie, forgetting that my mother was entertaining the ladies of the Bible Society, I placed my foot on the body of Numa the lion and uttered my cry. And the ladies leapt to their feet, teacups flying, faces blanched at the murder evidently taking place in the next room. But my mother was tranquil and reassuring. "Oh, that's all right," she said. "Pay it no mind. That's just Allen . . . practicing."

A TELEPHONE CALL from the nursing home. "Your mother is crawling around on the floor. We can't think what's got into her. Never been like this before. We pick her up, tie her in her chair, but first chance she gets she'll slip right out, sorta slide down, and then there she'll be, crawling around again." I ask the nurse to put her on the phone. After a while I hear the struggle, the labored breathing. "Hello, Mother. How are you?" Pause, then the thin, infinitely tired voice. "I guess I'm all right, son." I ask about the crawling. She begins to cry. "I've lost my rings."

THE WORLD is lost to her. Those rings were its vanishing point. When next I see her she still slides down out of her chair, gropes about on the floor, but no longer knows what she seeks. Everything is slipping away. She still has a grasp of me, though at times she stares blankly as if I too were fading.

The
Flying
Dutchman

Why, as I keep this vigil, do I keep thinking of the island in Puget Sound? Is that where I will die?

I remember a gleaming night last fall. I am lying in bed in darkness. I stretch, sink into luxurious softness, relax. Ilse is asleep beside me. The cedar branch waves sleepily before the window; the Sound is a ghostly silver under a cloudy sky. A sighing wind in the tall trees, the whisper of surf. I am suffused with a deep pleasure, happiness, a sense of power, of control. The long day just finished passes in review. Discontinuously. Click, click, click— like snapshots. Twenty hours earlier, at the beginning of this long day, I was lying in darkness, in just such a bed, not relaxed, but poised for flight. That was in Hotel

Margna, Sils Baselgia, in the Upper Engadin of Switzerland. It is just before five in the morning. I have, as always before a long journey, waked before the alarm clock sounds. Click, click, click. Going up the serpentine Julier Pass I catch a glimpse of a trailer truck coming down, two turns away, but coming too fast. I pull off the road and wait. As it roars by, brakes squealing, it occupies the entire road. Click, click, click. I am at the Air France counter in Zurich, waiting to check in. The line doesn't move. I sense a strange restlessness and inactivity in the staff; they are waiting for something. "There's going to be a strike," I whisper to my wife. "This plane won't leave." We move quickly, get the last two seats on a Swissair flight to Boston. Click, click, click. The camera focuses now on a moment six hours ago: On a winding road near Tacoma an oil rig passes me spilling oil. I stop. Other cars pass. "Why are we stopping?" my wife asks. Presently, up ahead, the cars spin out of control on the widening slick. I turn back, take a detour. Click, click, click. The camera is trained on the present moment. I am euphoric because of my quickness, my control of contingency. I glance at my sleeping wife. I have lofted her as on a perfectly aimed ballistic missile, halfway around the world, and there she is safe, asleep.

The Sound is a gleaming silver, the moon winks, and presently something other drifts in on the sighing wind. Click, click, click, this camera won't stop. I control nothing, am being swept away; a few more clicks and you'll search the frames for me in vain.

MY SISTER DEVELOPS Alzheimer's disease. Gradually her memory slips away. After a few years she knows nothing, can no longer feed herself or wipe her behind. Francis puts her in the nursing home alongside my mother. Neither recognizes the other. My sister wanders the hallways, smiles benignly, but does not speak. Francis dies of cancer; she knows nothing. She comes upon her mother down on the floor, stops and stares down at her with fixed and uncomprehending smile. My mother stops groping for her rings, glares up. "What is that woman doing here?" she cries angrily. "What does she want? Why is she staring at me? I don't like that! Something ought to be done about a situation like this! Where is the management? I'm going to report her!"

THE LIGHT snaps on. The nurse enters, opens the diaper. No feces now, just bright red blood. The nurse stares at me with a mute question: She wants to call an ambulance, wants my mother rushed to the hospital, to have a blood transfusion. I shake my head. She points to the hands and feet, which are turning blue. Again I shake my head. Her expression closes over with disapproval. She cleans my mother's wasted bottom, puts on a fresh diaper. Together, one on each side of the bed, we feel the pulse. It is weak and fast and thready. The nurse leaves.

SLOWLY MY EYES adapt to darkness. I see the faint line of gray molding around the ceiling. All is quiet. No bark of dog, no hum of traffic. Faint light of moon. It seems I have been running; I long to rest. I think of the island. It seems far away, long ago. Months ago. Yet, in fact, only days. A week ago we were there; we cleaned the house thoroughly as we always do, put everything away, locked up, left. It exists there now without us. Eight hundred miles away. Deserted, still, silent. Remote, dreamlike.

I call it back, I drift toward it, and presently it seems I am actually there. Moonlight on the moss-covered shakes; the white siding gleams brightly. I stand at the edge of the cliff. The Sound is still, a faint lapping at the shore below. The moon beats a straight wake from Mount Rainier across the water to me. Now I enter the house. I am a ghost, enter without unlocking or opening doors. Moonlight gleams on the polished oak floor. I pause to marvel at the vast depth of the silence. A scurrying sound in the chimney, and a chipmunk appears. Apparently I am neither seen nor felt, for the chipmunk moves calmly over, or perhaps through, my foot. The rug is rolled up and put away, all the cushions are in plastic bags, the wall hangings are in the closet, the thermostat is set at sixty degrees just as I left it. Everything cool, still. I pass through the closed door, walk down the path to the beach, sit in the sand, watch the moon rise in the sky, grow whiter, smaller.

The sky lightens. I walk back up the path. Now everything is different. Bright sunshine. People moving about. I see through the windows the wall hangings in place. An outdoor table has been set up; people are eating. Ah, I know this scene. This is Joan's birthday party two weeks ago. There I am sitting at the head of the table, facing, as always, down toward the orchard and the rugged Olympic Mountains to the north. All of my family is here. Ilse, Joan and her husband Pablo, Mark and his wife Katy and their children, Emily and Ian, Vicki and her sons Austin and Noah. And our old friends Phyllis and Otto. I watch myself sitting there, carving, pouring wine, eating, am amused to see myself thus, also somewhat uncomfortable, did not realize I was so stooped, so old and frail, in speech so modest, so uncertain.

My self at the table is unaware of my presence as a ghost. I walk about unseen, unheard, hear myself at the table saying those things I remember saying two weeks ago. And presently Emily, on request, sings her little song, "I'd rather have a Buick, a Buick," just as she did then.

I leave the festive scene, wander about the orchard. How I love this place! I walk up the sloping path to the mailboxes. An old woman is approaching, coming down the gravel road. Haggard face, stringy gray hair, slender, somewhat bent over but still quite tall. She limps slightly, but seems anyway to be hurrying, something of eagerness about her, of tense anticipation. Suddenly I realize that this is Mrs. Stringer. So she is a ghost too. Died about 1950. My house now was her house then. She left it to her son, Herbert Spahr. He sold it to me in 1962. All through the lonely Depression years, all through the heavy war years, Mrs. Stringer lived here alone. Phyllis would occasionally stop by. Hers was the only phone on the island, and she loved to have people come to use it. These were the only times she had anyone to talk to. The visitor would have to socialize a bit before using the phone, Mrs. Stringer would then eavesdrop on the call itself, and then there would be a little chat at the end. She was a great gossip.

She passes by me now and starts down the sloping path. Her pace slows. What once was an open sunny way is now a tunnel through arching trees. I see her shock as she notices that the barn is gone. There is nothing there. And a further shock on glancing to the right and seeing an enormous new barn where once was the old well. She walks on more slowly, shaken. The house at least will be as she remembers. It's not changed. But no, she looks in through the open front door, gives a start, decides not to enter, goes on around the corner of the house to where Joan's birthday party is in progress.

She stops suddenly, stands there searching the company. As her eyes rest on Phyllis I see a glimmer of recognition, which then fades. All are strange. She is looking for her son. Dismay deepens on her face. I see her lips form his name. No one hears. She knows no one. There is no place for her here. She turns to leave. At the corner of the house she pauses, looks back, moves on. I follow her. She is plodding up the path toward the mailboxes, stooped, tired, bereft. I feel for her, want to mitigate this usurpation. It *was* her home. I call, but she cannot hear. I take her arm, but she is as immaterial as I. No body, no contact, no comfort. She disappears in the dark of trees.

I am deeply troubled. She seemed to know that much time had passed, that things would be different. Yet still she hoped to find a place here. Her son would surely be here, and his children, whom she knew when they were little, and now, also, perhaps, her great-grandchildren, whom she would not know but who would look familiar. She would have a place. And that glance into the living room, that sudden not-entering. The wallpaper! Of course! Gone. She had picked it out herself, a great find. Dark green with pink flamingos, her great pride. She had pointed it out to everyone who stopped by to use the phone. I recall our own disdain. The first thing we did on acquiring this place was to rip it off, all of us, the whole family, stripping it away, vandalizing the room with a kind of scornful hilarity. We then paneled the walls with Philippine mahogany. That's why she didn't enter. It no longer looked like her house. And her son was not here. Only strangers.

As I come back around the corner of the house I sense a change. Yet there is the company of people around the table, the family party. But somehow everything is different. Suddenly I see that I am no longer sitting there at the head of the table. Someone else is in my place. And this is not my family! These are strangers. Adults and children. What are they doing here? An old woman in a wheelchair is off to one side. The others seem to ignore her. Something else is different. The tree at the edge of the cliff, the big Douglas fir. Where is it? It has disappeared as if by magic. Not a trace. The edge of the cliff itself has moved, is now six feet closer to the house. It would take fifty years for that much erosion. I walk down in the orchard. The trees are gone. I look for the green stone. The place is overgrown with salal and blackberry creepers. The stone is not to be found. I float back to the party. They have rolled the old lady onto the porch. Her withered hands flutter about the wheels; she wants to be with them, in the party, within the sound of human voices. Her eyes are milky with cataracts. My God! My daughter, Joan! My lissome child! I cry out, fall to the ground at her knees. She cannot hear me, cannot see me, I cannot reach her.

THE LAST TIME I came to visit, a few weeks ago, my mother was hallucinating.

"Oh! Oh! Look at that rain . . . how it's coming down. Close the window, son. Quick! Before everything is under water."

"It's all right, Mother. It's not raining. Nothing will get wet."

"The levee may not hold. See about the horses, son! . . . Mama! Mama!" She lifts herself slightly. "Where's my Mama, son?"

"She died a long time ago."

She falls back, sighs. "Ah yes. Ah yes. I remember now. . . . Araminta Matilde Black. Do you remember her? Poisoned her husband. . . . Said she didn't mean to, though. She was born in the spring during the high water and was buried on the banks of the Ouachita near Careyville. Smoke! Where is all that smoke coming from? Must be a terrible fire. I can't make out a thing. Gather up the valuables, son! Call the marshal!"

A DAY LATER.

"There's something wrong down here, son." She pushes at the bedclothes.

"Do you have pain?"

"No . . . a kind of itch, a burning."

"I'll ask the nurse to get you something."

"They don't know about such things. I've already told them. They don't know."

"Well, I'll ask your doctor."

"You're my doctor, son. Remember? You saved my life. Twice. If it weren't for you I wouldn't be here today." She has pushed down the covers, is pulling up her nightgown. "Have a look, son. See what you think."

"No, Mother, it's better that . . ."

"It's all right for you to look, son. You're a doctor."

She opens her legs, raises her knees. Her belly has disappeared, is draped against her spine; the aorta throbs visibly beneath the blotchy yellowish skin. Mons veneris has disappeared: no more that spongy rounded mound, no more that thicket of dark hair. A few spare tufts of white sprout from the bare bone of pubis. No flesh anywhere to be seen. The buttocks have vanished; the skin which once covered those ample cheeks now falls from the iliac crests as a gray curtain, pools on the sheet like candle wax. The bony architecture of the pelvis looms

up from the mattress like a ruined and haunted house—
of which I am the appalled ghost.

"Son . . . come closer. There's something we must talk
about." I sit on the edge of the bed. She takes my hand,
holds it between both her own, strokes it, looks away
into the distance. She is thinking, wants me to be prepared for a weighty matter. The bones of her hands are
covered with a yellowish film with dark brown blotches.
No flesh remains; the papery skin with its tangle of black
veins sinks in between the bones. "Son . . ." She focuses
on me, lowers her voice. "Son . . . we've been associated
together a long time. And so . . . it's only natural . . . that
we have become very *fond* of each other. It's been a very
long . . . and a very close . . . association. And so . . . after
all that time . . . it's only natural . . . we might want to get
married. . . ." She pauses. "We don't have to do it right
away, though. No need to rush into anything. But it's
only natural. . . ."

"I'm already married, Mother."

"You're already married?"

"Yes."

"Who is your wife? What is her *name,* son?"

"Ilse. . . . Do you remember Ilse?"

"Well . . . would she . . . be jealous?"

"Yes."

"Well . . . we certainly don't want to upset her. We
don't want that. We just won't rush into anything."

"Mother, listen! We *can't* get married. You're my
mother, I'm your *son!"*

"Yes . . . well . . . that's true, that's certainly true, and we've been very close, very close together . . . for a very long time. That's true, isn't it?"

"Yes."

"But we don't want to upset anyone. We mustn't cause a stir. But I want to tell you something, son." She strokes my hand tenderly. "We have plenty of time. No need to rush into anything. So . . . if you want to look around first, try out some of the younger girls . . . see how you like it . . . if you want to do that . . . I want you to know, I won't mind. You look around all you like. I'll wait for you."

HER BREATHING now is a labored rattle. The legs are blue to above the knees, the arms to above the elbows. I cannot feel a pulse.

THE ASTONISHED BIRD flies upward, high, high, away from its strangely burning feet. Alights on a telephone wire, falls forward, with spread wings catches itself, flies to the branch of a tree, falls forward, tries again, falls, and again, again. Now it flutters motionless in air, hovers like an osprey above a branch, lowers itself vertically, with a beating of wings, touches down, falls backward, flutters to another branch, falls forward. Presently it alights on a shelf of leaves, finds itself resting, but not on its feet; the legs without feet have dropped between the twigs. The wings beat helplessly against the leaves. Presently it falls clear, again is airborne, alights on a branch, falls forward, to another, falls, falls, falls. Trees and earth have become hostile. Now it soars up, up, as if to leave them behind, to find another realm, high in the darkening sky. But is getting weak, cannot sustain itself, is drifting down again to resume its agony. The swoops from branch to branch become shorter, lower. Presently it drops to the top of a bush, finds itself enmeshed in branches. It cannot move. Children play nearby, mothers call; it is time to go home. The bird flutters, drops deeper in the bush, is trapped. A dog hears the flutter, is sniffing; a black nose pushes its way into the bush. The wings flutter violently; the bird drops lower and lower. The dog sniffs. Presently the bird fights clear of the lowest branches, falls to the ground. The nose is upon it, the whiskers quiver, the nostrils dilate. The dog's eyes, intent with curiosity, are without malice, without pity, without mercy. The mouth opens on large teeth. The frantic bird flutters, rolls; the dog follows. Presently the wings gain the air, carry the bird again aloft and away from the open mouth. It flies up to a branch, falls, catches itself, to another, falls, and if one could follow the path of this desperate bird through the darkening afternoon one would find hundreds of branches marked with two tiny red dots.

It is weak now, cannot fly up, alights on the bar of a children's turnabout, falls, hits the platform with a thud, rolls to the sand. It flutters this way and that, zigzag, out of the sand, gains the air, but cannot rise. It flies a foot or so above the ground, alights on a concrete walk, falls forward, beak hitting the stone. Again and again it flies and alights, again and again the beak striking the stone.

The eyes are glazed; a trickle of blood runs from the beak. The flutter of wings subsides, is finally still. It is night. A rising wind stirs the feathers.

I DRIVE SLOWLY through the cemetery. Winter. A cold clear day, blue sky, weak noonday sun. The trees are barren, the grass dry and withered. The gray stones gleam dully, strewn as if at random in the sloping brown meadow. In the distance a hearse, a black-suited man waiting nearby. He notices my hesitation, starts toward me. I stop the car. We get out, I introduce my family, he leads the way. We come to a blue awning mounted on poles, open on all sides, covering the grave. I recognize the coffin I selected at the funeral home. It rests on green canvas slings within a chrome frame. Beneath the frame a green carpet simulating grass. We approach. "Not too close," the director cautions. I sense the black void beneath the fake grass. We stand in silence before the casket. Beside my feet is a flat gray stone:

DR. A. B. WHEELIS

1882–1925

The director whispers to me: "Shall I . . . ?" I nod. He opens the upper segment of the casket lid.

On a billowy white bed lies my mother, exposed to us now from the waist up. She wears a striped silk blouse that my wife bought for her years ago. Her head is elevated on a white ruffled pillow, her white hair nicely combed, her face powdered and rouged. Her mouth and eyes are closed. The lines of care and of anxiety have been wiped smooth. We stare at her. "She looks more serene in death," I say, "than ever in life." We shift about slightly, uneasily, but remain facing her. The funeral director appears again; he wants to know if others will be coming, perhaps a minister. "No one else," I say, then add, "We will stand here awhile . . . and talk." He nods, retreats. After a while I begin to speak.

"I want to say something . . . in tribute to my mother . . . lest those qualities of hers deserving of tribute be lost. And they *might* be lost, for they were not much in evidence in recent years. In 1947 . . . she had a long and serious illness . . . almost died . . . never fully recovered. She was fifty-eight. That's when she began to be old. And she became . . . finally . . . a foolish and pathetic old woman. Foolish in her doting . . . and erotized . . . adoration of me, and . . . in her constant exaggeration of my virtues and my accomplishments. And mean-spirited in her invidious denigration of my sister."

I am speaking softly, with long unintended pauses, as if wanting someone to break in. The four others incline their heads slightly toward me.

"But once the colors of her life were more vivid. And that's what I want to recall . . . and to evoke."

That's not true, I think; the colors of her life were always gray.

"Her father was a man of immense authority . . . in his community and in . . . his family. And no one was more respectful of that authority than my mother. But when she fell in love she found the strength to oppose him. 'I forbid you to marry this man,' her father said. 'He will never have anything, and he will die young of tuberculosis.' As it turned out he was right . . . on both counts. But my mother followed her heart. Because of her father's opposition, she could not be married at home or even in the same town. But one day my father pulled up in a buggy, and my mother walked out of her father's house and they drove off to Farmersville and were married by the justice of the peace. So . . . one must say of her . . . she was a woman capable of independent action."

That, too, is a lie. Why am I standing here with my family telling lies? Never on her own did she defy her father. When *my* father came along and she fell in love, she simply transferred her dependence to him; and on *his* authority, in obedience to *his* will, walked out of her father's house.

"And in 1937 in Marion a black man named Norris was beaten by Joe Turner, the farmer who employed him. Norris had left the gate open, and the cows had got into the garden . . . and Joe Turner was a man with a bad temper. At that time, in that place, a black man did not fight back, for that would invite a lynching. He just took it—stoically or perhaps begging for mercy. So Norris stood and took his beating: broken jaw, missing teeth, broken shoulder. The town regarded such an incident with tolerance—amused tolerance by some ('That'll teach ole Norris a lesson! Guess it'll be a spell 'fore he leaves that gate open agin!'), disapproving tolerance by others. The sheriff certainly wasn't going to do anything about it. My mother tried to get my Uncle Kleber to act, but he didn't want to tangle with Joe Turner. So nothing was done. But one day . . . on a Saturday about noon . . . in the middle of the town square . . . with people milling about . . . my mother accosted Joe Turner. 'I know what you did,' she said, 'and it was an evil and dastardly thing. This town, it looks like, will do nothing about it, but I hope God will punish you.' And so . . . she was a woman capable of acting alone . . . on principle."

I wasn't there. That's the story. Mit told me. Perhaps there's something to it. I made up the words, but perhaps she did say something, maybe not at noon, not in the town square, maybe not even to Joe Turner directly, but *something*. Every life holds some myth of heroism, and I credit hers with this brave confrontation.

"When my mother and father got married, my father was deep in debt for his medical school education, and during their first years together they had to pay this off. They were very poor. During those years, also, they had three children, one of whom died. And then, in 1917, just when things might have begun to be easier for them, the war started and my father entered the army. My mother followed him, with her children, to camps in Alabama and to Chattanooga, Tennessee. In 1918 he had the flu, but recovered—or so he thought—and in 1919 was out of the army. They settled then in the town of Minden, near Marion. He bought equipment, opened an office—and now, they thought, things would get easier. But within months he was down with tuberculosis.

"He was advised to go west and chose San Antonio,

and my mother went with him. Since his illness was service-connected, he could have remained indefinitely in a veterans' hospital, but my mother knew that he would have a better chance at home. So she rented a house and brought him home and nursed him. For six years . . . she cooked for him, brought his meals, bathed him, dressed him, burned the sputum cups, carried the bedpans, and boiled the sheets of his bed in an iron pot over a wood fire in the backyard. And all this, while taking care also of her children—in good spirit and without complaint. And so . . . one must say of her, she was a woman capable of unusual loyalty . . . and devotion . . . and self-sacrifice."

All this is true. Finally . . . something I'm saying is true.

"And when, one October morning, just after daybreak . . . yellow sunlight streaming in horizontally through the windows, glinting off my father's upturned and now waxen face . . . everyone waiting . . . speechless, breathless . . . the doctor straightened up, folded his stethoscope, and said, 'He's gone,' there burst forth from my mother's throat a scream . . . so loud . . . so terrifying . . . the sound of a large animal that has been struck a mortal blow . . . a scream that tore through me like a spear . . . and she reeled back, flailing wildly, falling . . . and a few days later . . . at this very spot . . . her anguished sobs as his body was lowered. And so . . . one must say of her . . . she was a woman capable of passion and of pain."

Of pain certainly. Of pain there was a lot. Of passion

I'm not so sure. Passion and desire she ascribed to men, making of herself an object, the obedient and responsive object of the will of her father, her husband, and her son. Of these three I had her the longest, am therefore most responsible for the shape of her life.

I end in a whisper, look about at my family. They are huddled around me, heads inclined toward me. They have been hanging in my net of words. Now that I have stopped they are falling anxiously inward.

I signal to the funeral director that we are ready. He starts to close the casket. My wife takes my arm: "I want to say something." She fumbles, finds the pocket, extracts a piece of paper. I motion to the director to wait. "As I was thinking . . ." She bursts into tears. Presently, after a pause, she makes a new start. "As I was thinking what words to speak today four lines from a Chinese poem came to mind.

> "Man lives but once
> and never he returns.
> Life is like a breath of air
> that wafts away.

"But only our bodies don't return—so there will be room for others to live and to remember." Tears are streaming down her face. "Therefore I want to mourn Grandma's death by celebrating the lives of those who will contain her memory—her much-loved son, my husband, and our wonderful children, her grandchildren. May you live long and remember her fondly."

Mark, weeping, says a few words. Vicki, dry-eyed, speaks briefly. We stand in silence. I glance at Joan. She looks strained, choked; her eyes are large and shining. She shakes her head. Again I signal to the director that we are ready. Again he starts to close the casket. Joan whispers to me something I don't understand. "What?" She takes my arm, brings her mouth to my ear: "Her head is too high." Still I don't understand. She points to the white satin above my mother's face: "It's hitting her *nose!*" I see then a smudge of makeup on the white lining of the casket lid. My daughter Joan! In matters of this kind the unchallenged Mistress of Protocol. When her goldfish died she positioned the tiny glittering body in water, in seaweed, in the exact horizontal, as if still alive and swimming; and her hamster in death was arranged in his box in the exact posture in which, in life, it had slept. We are delivering the body of her grandmother to the worms, but so long as it is in our care she will not permit that nose to be crowded.

At my request the funeral director rearranges the pillow, lowers my mother's head, then closes the casket.

We are asked to move back. Workmen appear, lift the chrome frame, slide out the green carpet. The grave yawns below—clean-cut walls of black earth, cut roots. Six feet down is an open concrete box, approximating the walls of the grave. The workmen bend to the winches. The chrome rollers turn, the green canvas sling unrolls, the coffin descends jerkily. A workman with a slender pole guides the casket into the box. With a muted thud it comes to rest. The slings are freed and withdrawn, the chrome frame removed. We stand at the edge, staring down.

"I'm afraid this will be noisy," the funeral director says, and moves us back. A gas engine starts up with a rattling clatter, and a small tractor comes chugging toward us pushing a wheeled frame within which is suspended a flat concrete slab. The frame is maneuvered over the grave. The winch turns; the lid is lowered, guided into position. The body within the coffin, within the concrete box, is now twice removed from us, is being sealed further and further away.

Again we are asked to move back. The tent is struck, poles and lines are stashed, the canvas folded, loaded into a cart. Pale winter sunlight falls around us, the pale winter sky spreads out above. Again the start-up of a motor, again the chugging tractor, this time pulling a dumpster of black soil. It maneuvers with difficulty between the stones, backs the dumpster to the edge of the grave. Here now, without deceptive green, is the hidden piano of sixty-five years ago. The player has vanished, the melody is lost. I am given a shovel. I reach up over the edge of the cart, take a shovelful of dirt. After a moment of hesitation, staring down, I deliver the soil. It swishes softly on the concrete slab. I take some slight comfort that the coffin itself is shielded from this falling earth. My wife follows, then each of my tall children, each in turn with a shovelful of earth.